# Funding Justice

## The Legacy of the Unitarian Universalist Veatch Program

Warren Ross

SKINNER HOUSE BOOKS
BOSTON

Copyright © 2005 by Warren Ross. All rights reserved. Published by
Skinner House Books, an imprint of the Unitarian Universalist Association.
The Unitarian Universalist Association is a liberal religious organization with
more than one thousand congregations in the United States and Canada.
25 Beacon Street, Boston, MA 02108-2800.

Printed in the United States.

Cover design by Kimberly Glyder.

ISBN 1-55896-494-0
    978-1-55896-494-5

Library of Congress Cataloging-in-Publication Data

Ross, Warren.
  Funding Justice : the legacy of the Unitarian Universalist Veatch Program /
Warren Ross.
       p. cm.
  Includes bibliographical references (p.  )
  ISBN 1-55896-494-0 (alk. paper)
  1. Church finance 2.  Unitarian Universalist Veatch Program.
  QA76.73.J38J356 2005
  3. Unitarian Universalist churches—Finance. 4.  Church and social problems—
Unitarian Universalist churches. 5. Unitarian Universalist Congregation of
Shelter Rock (Manhasset, N.Y.) I.  Title.
  BV774.5.R67 2005
  267'.189132—dc22
  2005002985


10 9 8 7 6 5 4 3 2 1
10 09 08 07 06 05


Photographs provided by the Veatch Program and reprinted with the permis-
sion of the Veatch Program and grant recipients.
This book funded in part with grants from the Fund for Unitarian Universalism.

This book is dedicated to the Unitarian Universalist Congregation at Shelter Rock, New York, whose vision and generosity have made possible the achievements of the Veatch Program, and to the volunteers and staff who have worked hard for half a century to ensure its continued success.

# Contents

# Foreword

MEMBERS OF THE Unitarian Universalist Congregation at Shelter Rock have been blessed by the bequest of Caroline Veatch that continues to fund our Veatch Program. Because we did not raise these funds ourselves—or provide them out of our own pockets—we feel a special obligation to share them widely.

Our service on the Veatch board of governors is a way to live up to that obligation, and we are grateful for this opportunity to put our religious principles into practice.

Beginning in the late 1950s, our congregation started using some of the Veatch income to support the Unitarian Universalist denomination and to provide building loans for churches across the country. In the late 1960s, as the royalty income grew, we became more professional and intentional in our giving. New strategies were forged during a decade of activism by many members of the congregation around civil rights, antiwar efforts, affordable housing, and other issues.

What was once a program committee was reconstituted as a board. Over the past forty years, in addition to supporting the Unitarian Universalist Association and its affiliate organizations, this Veatch board, backed by the congregation, expanded its mission to fund nondenominational not-for-profit organizations working for social justice on local, regional, and national issues. As the grant acceptance letter makes clear, "The Unitarian Universalist Congregation at Shelter Rock has made this grant because the work that you will undertake with our financial support will, in the opinion of the Veatch board, strengthen and further the goals of Unitarian Universalism."

The members of our church are proud of this tradition—not only as it is reflected in actions of the Veatch Program, but also as exhibited in the overall dedication of the congregation to social activism. It is important work we are able to do, not as a relief or social service organization—important as those are—but as a religious community addressing the root causes of our society's problems: why there are not enough jobs; why people are going hungry; why the economy and the environment are under stress; why even our very democracy is under stress. We try to address these systemic problems as effectively as possible, often in collaboration with other progressive funders.

Our motivation and encouragement in these efforts derive from our Unitarian Universalist principles. Our most important value is the concept of community. While there is also a lot of emphasis on individualism in our tradition, what inspires us most is the principle that we are part of a larger whole, part of the web of all existence, and that what happens to any one of us affects all of us. Therefore we need to be concerned about everyone and everything, about all humanity and all of nature.

We truly believe that if everyone would embrace the principles we foster it would be a much better world, and Veatch's work would not be needed. But, unfortunately, that is not realistic. To the modest extent we can, we try to influence this nation's direction in order to sustain the democratic ideals to which we, as a religious community, aspire. To accomplish this, we fund nonreligious, liberal organizations that are working to uphold the same ideals and have the specialized capacity to meet particular goals. That is the mission of the Veatch Program, and with the help of our invaluable staff, we do our best to carry it forward.

Zed Kesner and Carol Adams
Immediate Past Chair and Chair
Veatch Program Board of Governors
April 2005

# Preface

I T WAS A privilege to be asked to tell the story of the Veatch Program. I knew of it, of course, having served on the board of the Unitarian Universalist Association at a time when Veatch funds literally saved the association. Also, I knew that its grants give critical support to grassroots organizations devoted to social justice and the democratic process. But not until I heard from these grant recipients directly did I get an understanding of just how vital a contribution Veatch has been making to the preservation and furtherance of our democratic values.

The way I went about gathering the information on which this book is based was first to study the records generously made available by the Veatch board of governors. That, however, was the end of their involvement. Next I conducted some fifty interviews—about half in person and half by phone—starting with Veatch staff and volunteers, continuing with denominational officials, and then talking to those who are putting Veatch grants to work to improve their communities and causes. While that meant reaching only a minority of grant recipients, with the help of the Veatch staff, especially Marjorie Fine, the executive director, I endeavored to make sure that my sample was representative of the types of organizations Veatch supports.

The interviews were conducted during 2003. That means they are snapshots in time: Some of those interviewed may have changed jobs; some of the grants may not have been renewed now that the Veatch Program has had to cut its budget. The essence of what is being reported on, however, has not changed, and that essence should serve as a source of inspiration for all who share the vision that underlies our liberal religious principles.

W. R.
April 2005

# The Founding of the Veatch Program

BECAUSE OF ITS tremendous impact on the Unitarian Universalist Association (UUA) and many other aspects of Unitarian Universalist life and thought, not to mention the denomination's standing in the world at large, many Unitarian Universalists will have heard of "Veatch." It is unlikely, however, that more than a few know just how significant the Veatch Program has been in sustaining UU ideals and principles—or even how it got its name. That alone makes this a story worth knowing, but there is also a personal reason that should resonate with the readers: they may gain hope and inspiration from the way the devoted people on both the giving and receiving ends of Veatch generosity have demonstrated how to make this a better world.

Although popularly referred to simply as Veatch, the full, formal name is the Veatch Program of the Unitarian Universalist Congregation at Shelter Rock. Parsing that mouthful explains much of where the money comes from, the principles that determine how it is spent, and how a single congregation has steadfastly dedicated itself to the faithful stewardship of unexpected riches.

The story begins with the late Caroline Veatch. Her generosity some half a century ago continues to underwrite the program that honors her memory—though at the time she made her bequest no one could have foreseen just how fruitful its impact would

1

eventually become. To explain this evolution requires a brief recap of the history of the Unitarian Universalist Congregation at Shelter Rock.

The congregation is the descendant of the North Shore Unitarian Society, located first in Port Washington and later in Plandome on New York's Long Island. When the congregation outgrew both of these locations, the congregation moved to Shelter Rock Road in nearby Manhasset. By that time, the American Unitarian Association had merged with the Universalist Church of America, so the congregation was renamed to reflect both its new location and the new name of the denomination. What has not changed over the course of this history is the remarkable tradition of generosity the congregation established when the originally modest income from the Caroline Veatch bequest first exceeded its own needs.

Success, it is said, has many parents. In the case of the Veatch Program this is not just a metaphor but a verifiable fact. Among those who deserve recognition for their seminal roles are Rev. Gerald Weary, first minister, and the lay leaders of the then just recently (1945) founded religious society.

When Weary started making parish calls, Julia Wagner, a member of the congregation who was giving Caroline Veatch physical therapy, suggested that he visit her. Wagner told Weary that Caroline was a widow who, being homebound, was unable to attend services, but who had expressed an interest in the new congregation. In his memoir, Weary says that he called on "Carrie," as he refers to her, even before he had conducted his first service, and for the next eight years he, and sometimes his wife, visited Caroline Veatch at least every other week. After about two years, he recalls in his memoirs, she "initiated a conversation with me about remembering the Society in her will," and she mentioned that the royalty rights to German oil fields that her geologist husband had left her were—one Great Depression and one World War later—just beginning to become productive.

Having joined the church, Mrs. Veatch asked Weary whether there was an attorney in the congregation who would be willing to help her with her will and also to find out how she could obtain her royalties, which were blocked by legal and currency complications. If the attorney succeeded, she promised, she would give half the earnings to the congregation. After two years of sorting out lost records and conflicting claims, James Nickerson, church member and senior partner in a large New York City law firm, succeeded and, Weary's memoir continues, "On January 14, 1952, Jim received from Germany a remittance in United States dollars of $7,168, and turned it over to Carrie, who, in turn . . . gave one-half to the North Shore Unitarian Society." What's more, she agreed to share her income while she lived and to deed the royalty income to the church upon her death.

Grateful as he was for her gift, Weary little imagined how this modest amount would multiply into a monetary avalanche. When Caroline Veatch died in October 1953, the congregation received not only the royalty income but some $50,000 in cash and 35,000 shares in the North European Oil company that her husband had founded, but which were sold before anyone suspected their potential value.

Slowly the royalty income began to mount. By the late 1960s, when Harvey Cohen joined the board, he expressed surprise that no one had ever gone to Germany to check on the congregation's rights, whereupon he was authorized to make the trip. Going a second time two years later, in 1970, he met with the German lawyer and oil geologist who were looking after the interests of the church, trying to unravel just exactly what the congregation was entitled to. One problem was that its deeds had disappeared in the war—some say bombed, some say burned. Another critical issue was the dispute as to whether the royalties should be based on production at the wellhead or on revenues at the distribution point.

A further problem was that the German government was taking half the revenues for taxes. Among the many church leaders who deserve credit for the bonanza to come is Robert Adelman, who was instrumental in getting the U.S.–West German tax treaty amended so that the society's Veatch income was no longer taxable in Germany. With these issues resolved and with natural gas replacing oil as the primary source of profits, the flow of royalty income rapidly began to swell. In the 1971–1972 fiscal year it totaled $577,000. The following year it leaped to over $10 million. The next three years' income climbed to about $20 million. Since then, the income has fluctuated from year to year and recently has begun to decline, but it has continued to exceed the congregation's own needs. This led to some critical decisions that shaped what became the Veatch Program and, indirectly, the future of the entire denomination.

## Sharing the Wealth

Unexpected riches bring out the true character of sudden million-aires. Some fritter away the money and wind up broke; some invest it wisely; a few become philanthropists. Congregations face the same challenge, and it would have been easy for the North Shore Society to become ingrown, protective of its wealth, or even to waste it. Instead a group of visionary leaders developed what might be called the Veatch concept. Alan Doran, Malcolm and Eleanor Vendig, Harlow Lincoln, Philip Dalsimer, Harvey Cohen, Robert Adelman, Ed Lawrence, and many others, staunchly supported by Rev. Harold Hadley, their longtime minister, set up and guided the Caroline Veatch Assistance and Extension Program. They could not have done it, of course, without the support of the entire membership, and in 1959 the congregation adopted a resolution that says in part, "It is thought that the establishment of a program for existing Unitarian Fellowships and Churches and other Unitarian programs through loans and/or gifts which are designed to foster and promote Unitarianism will be a worthy program in its own right and one which will suitably and appropriately honor Caroline Veatch." It passed with fifty-five votes to three, with three abstentions. The resolution also set up a Veatch

Committee of five church members to set policies and recommend loans to be ratified by the church board of trustees.

At first, Veatch funds were mostly used to make loans and gifts to other Unitarian congregations, primarily on Long Island. One received $1,000 for lights, another $500 for bridge tables. And the denomination—which had helped the North Shore Society get established through a building loan—was not forgotten. This support also started modestly, with a 1958 grant of $13,700 to the American Unitarian Association (AUA) for the recruitment of ministers. Contributions also went to the Unitarian (later Unitarian Universalist) Service Committee, the denomination's United Nations Office, and the International Association for Religious Freedom, among others.

This precedent was adhered to even as the ground-shifting discovery of natural gas wells vastly enlarged Veatch resources. Nor did it take long for word of the bonanza to spread. Having initially decided to concentrate on stimulating Unitarian growth on Long Island, the committee soon received (and usually turned down) applications from as far away as Illinois, Texas, and North Carolina.

## Growing Pains

But giving away money is not easy, and as the congregation was flooded with requests it soon became apparent that the administration of such sizable funds was beyond the scope of a volunteer committee. The first paid staff member was Eleanor Vendig as loan administrator. Upon his retirement, Ed Lawrence, by then the committee chair, was prevailed upon to take over as part-time executive director. Vendig and Lawrence worked together for nearly twenty years.

But not only did the administration evolve to keep pace with the inflow of money; so did the basic criteria for its disbursement. "Ed and I used to commute together," Robert Adelman, then the church board president recalls, "and I kept after him to make the grants bigger." "Let's not buy new card tables—let's really make a difference," he remembers saying.

There also was a controversy. Church member James Regan acted as legal counsel to the Veatch Committee, and when a request came to support the Family Service Association of Nassau County, he ruled that state law precluded giving money to nondenominational groups. According to Robert Sunley, chair of the congregation's Archives and History Committee (on whose records and publications much of this account is based), Mal Vendig "strenuously objected," citing other lawyers who argued the opposite. The dispute was referred to the board of trustees, which listened to both Regan and Vendig, and when they sided with Vendig, Regan resigned as counsel and walked out.

With this issue resolved, the Veatch Program established the two-pronged approach to grantmaking that is still its guiding principle today. The first emphasis is to support programs that foster the growth and development of the denomination and increase the involvement of Unitarian Universalists in social action. The second is to support grassroots organizations whose goals reflect the principles of Unitarian Universalism, with special emphasis on promoting justice, equity, and compassion in human relations, and strengthening the democratic process. In line with these principles, here is how the Veatch Program recently defined itself:

> Much is wrong in the world as we find it in the beginning of the twenty-first century. Tremendous greed exists alongside unbearable poverty. . . . We believe that fundamental changes are needed—changes in values, in priorities, in analysis, and in governance.

> We also believe that these changes will occur only if the people of this country themselves provide the leadership that is so sorely lacking. The Veatch Program funds organizations of people, not of "experts," because we believe that it is only by rebuilding democracy in this country from the bottom up that truly new policies will be envisioned, demanded, and implemented.

Considering how many volatile issues Veatch grants have touched on, internal conflicts and outside criticism have been relatively rare, but by no means absent. The raw emotions of the Vietnam War, for instance, caused ripples within the congregation when the Toronto Interfaith Council applied for support of its efforts to help U.S. citizens who fled to Canada to escape the draft. Seeking to avoid a split in the congregation, the Veatch Committee recommended that the UU Service Committee study this need. Eventually, by a vote of three to one, the committee voted to approve a matching grant—the full amount to be contingent on contributions by individual church members. It was an ingenious solution at a time when even the bold learned to be cautious.

## Perfecting the Process

One structural change remained to be made to achieve the current Veatch organizational model. After all, with no precedent to go on, the program was inventing itself as it went along, or as Ed Lawrence admitted, "Only experience will tell us what is right." One problem that experience uncovered was that requiring the church board to approve each grant proved extremely burdensome. It meant, as Sunley commented, that the time needed to study, discuss, and decide on each loan or grant proposal "pushed aside or delayed other board business," or as Lawrence put it, "The board was spending its time giving away money instead of running a church."

After a report by a study committee and considerable debate, it was decided to transform the Veatch Committee into a Veatch board of governors, to be elected by the congregation. One of the alternatives considered was setting up a separate foundation, but this suggestion was quickly rejected when it was realized that this might jeopardize the German tax exemption. Instead, it was made clear that the Veatch Program remained an integral part of the church, but that the new board would have the right to approve all grants up to $50,000. Larger amounts would have to be ratified by the congregation—not the board of trustees. And, of course, the congregation would continue to vote on the yearly allocation to the Veatch Program. Another part of the revamping was provision for a professional staff headed by a full-time executive director, and Lawrence was named to this position pro tem, soon to be made permanent.

This structure prevails today. Veatch now has a staff of seven, including three program officers. They review some one thousand grant applications per year and forward the ones they approve of to the executive director, who in turn submits them to the Veatch board of governors, which has the final say. Thus the church board of trustees is free to concentrate on the congregation's business, and the volunteer members of the board of governors quickly develop expertise in reviewing grant proposals and setting overall policy.

This process involves many phone calls and exchanges of e-mail, a dialogue that continues throughout the life of the two hundred or so grants that are approved each year. If the grantees live up to their plans and reporting obligations and appear to be achieving their objectives, many of the grants are renewed. As David Fleischer of the National Gay and Lesbian Taskforce explains, Veatch forms a partnership relationship with its grant recipients:

> Veatch and the UU Congregation at Shelter Rock have made some very unusual and admirable choices. Their animating philosophy has been to think seriously about how to reduce the divisions in our society that polarize us and keep us from understanding each other in our common humanity. Ultimately, people will look back on what they have accomplished and applaud them not just for being important and wise, but courageous.

It is a sentiment repeatedly echoed by other grant recipients. As for the role Veatch has played in supporting the denomination, past-UUA President Robert West offers this assessment:

It would be to difficult to exaggerate the contribution of the Plandome congregation in enabling our Unitarian Universalist Association to continue as an effective liberal religious continental denomination. In an era of deep and divisive crises, the congregation through its Veatch Program acted quietly and responsibly to maintain valuable programs and underwrite new approaches to cope with the problems that beset our religious movement. The congregation's contribution to our Unitarian Universalist denomination and its continuance is of inestimable worth and benefit, for which we and our descendants should remain profoundly grateful.

The Veatch Program has won a unique reputation not only within the denomination but also in the field of progressive philanthropy, indeed the wider philanthropic field. David Hunter, a foundation executive, paraphrasing a speech delivered at the National Council of Foundations, describes Veatch as "a model for many long-established philanthropic enterprises." One of the reasons it is so good, he says, "is that it keeps examining itself, it keeps open to new perspectives . . . it doesn't let itself get petrified." Specifically, he praises the Veatch Program's dedication to freedom of speech and thought, its willingness to help controversial ideas get expressed, and its courage in the face of manifest threats. He adds that because of Veatch's willingness to question orthodox assumptions, it has "a great deal to say to the rest of us involved in giving away money." Such success is all the more remarkable considering that Veatch cannot compare with the giants in the foundation field in resources or size; it is sizable only in terms of our denomination and by comparison with its modest beginning. But while the scope of the Veatch Program has grown far beyond its founders' dreams, the impulse that made the congregation decide to share its wealth to promote liberal religious institutions and ideals still permeates all its activities.

# Helping the Helpers
## *The Grantmaker Coalitions*

WHILE THE VEATCH Program's two major areas of emphasis are, first, support of Unitarian Universalist activities and organizations and, second, funding organizations that actively promote UU principles, its influence has also been felt in a third area: providing leadership in building coalitions of progressive funding organizations.

Mainstream philanthropies such as the Kellogg or Rockefeller Foundations support many constructive activities in such areas as education, healthcare, and medical research. With a few exceptions, however, they have little stomach for controversy. Hence "troublemakers" need not apply—and grassroots organizations that challenge the status quo often need to make what the powerful and complacent consider trouble to reach their goals. Organizations that challenge the system, therefore, need to turn to smaller, more venturesome funders such as the Veatch Program for support and, to maximize their effectiveness, these progressive funders have joined together in such groups as the National Network of Grantmakers; Interfaith Funders; Grassroots Institute for Fundraising Training; and the Alliance for Justice. Veatch has not only supported them with grants but, through its board members and staff, has provided them with catalytic leadership.

11

## It Pays to Network

The National Network of Grantmakers has a staff of just two, plus two consultants, but while small, it is quite influential in making community organizing more effective. Nicole Trombley, the Network's acting executive director, describes its mission this way:

> Our members come together around a common vision: to move more money to social and economic justice work. To that end we bring to the table private foundations, family foundations, community-based foundations, religious giving programs, corporate funders, and other types of independent grant makers.

The Network is a membership organization made up not of organizations, but of individuals associated with those organizations. Veatch Program staff and board members have been active participants for many years. Marjorie Fine, for example, has chaired committees, led workshops, and served as a member and officer of the board.

According to Trombley, the work of the Network's members is not just about "moving checks." Because of their shared sense of mission and their understanding of the role of progressive philanthropy, they are trying to build movements for social and economic justice in many other ways as well: "They realize that they also need to play a role in harnessing the rest of philanthropy, and to advocate with their colleagues in the foundation field to mobilize more resources for the grassroots groups they support."

While in past years the Network has encouraged its members to be more generous in allocating their funds, the problem today is often how to cope with shrinking resources. The Veatch Program, for example, experienced a budget cut of nearly a million dollars (roughly 10 percent) in 2004, and the ripple effect of the recent economic downturn has been that virtually all endowments have taken substantial hits. As Trombley points out, "not only has there been a sense of economic crisis on the part of the grantmakers, but the community organizations they support are really nervous about their ability to meet their budgets. Most of them don't have endowments, so they rely on fundraising every year, and that's tough when people are worried about their jobs or may even be unemployed."

There is another worry besetting Network members in recent times: the political climate in which they operate. As Trombley puts it,

> Since 9/11, people are really worried about the shift to the right the country is taking. The rolling back of civil liberties under the Patriot Act is only one of the issues. Overall, many of our members fund small organizations that by mainstream standards could be considered radical or extremist, even though in actual fact they are grassroots groups doing good work. But it's a very slippery line as to who could be accused of being terrorist, and you've got to worry about where that line is going to be drawn.

## Interfaith Funders

Another alliance of progressive grantmakers in which Veatch participates is called Interfaith Funders (IF), which brings up another recent political concern.

The Bush Administration's efforts to channel government money to religious groups that share its political agenda has thrown a cloud of ambiguity over the term "faith-based." Any discussion of faith-based community organizations must therefore start with this disclaimer: These economic and social justice groups neither receive nor are ever likely to receive government support. What many of them do receive is Veatch support, and it's easy to see why.

IF participants see that their primary role is not to provide services (though some do), but to develop participants' leadership skills, build a strong web of relationships through congregations and other institutions, and turn those relationships into a civic power capable of making change to promote the public good. The IF statement goes on to say that this approach to community organizing is gathering strength:

> A force for democracy is growing in the United States. The uninvolved are participating, the voiceless are speaking, and the powerful are beginning to listen. Marginalized people in countless neighborhoods across thirty-three states are influencing the decision-making institutions that control their quality of life. Blacks, whites, Hispanics, and Asians are rolling up their sleeves to secure living wages, affordable housing, safe neighborhoods, and much more for their families and communities.

Many but by no means all of these approximately four thousand groups have close relationships with local congregations, and often are supported by their respective denominations or by denominational social justice affiliates. As the statement continues,

> Faith-based community organizing (FBCO) groups bring people together through their congregations, but also through their unions, community organizations, and children's schools. The vast majority of FBCO groups are made up of racially diverse institutions, and involve congregations from different religious traditions. . . . Because [faith-based organizing] is grounded in the values and traditions that come from religious faith, it is also sometimes called values-based organizing. But whatever you call it, FBCO is a growing force.

There are some 134 faith-based community organizing networks that belong to Interfaith Funders. Along with the Veatch Program they include the Catholic Campaign for Human Development; the Jewish Fund for Justice; the Domestic Hunger Program of the Evangelical Lutheran Church in America; and the One Great Hour of Sharing Fund of the Presbyterian Church USA. While each network differs in emphasis, they all help new local groups get started;

promote the sharing of information, strategies, and tactics; provide ongoing training and mentoring to their organizers and leaders; and help to identify specific issues to target.

Again, the Veatch involvement in Interfaith Funders goes beyond money. Marjorie Fine is a member of the board and, according to IF's executive director Jeannie Appleman, has been a key person in the organization and a participant in what Appleman calls collaborative grantmaking. "Margie Fine," she explains, "sits on our grantmaking committee, so she's at the table along with the representatives of the Catholic Campaign for Human Development and other member organizations, and they decide together what groups IF is going to support. That means a lot of networking is going on, because they have so much in common."

They don't necessarily conclude that they will all give grants to the same organizations, since each group has its own funding priorities. IF, for example, will fund only faith-based groups, while Veatch looks for other ways, too, to promote Unitarian Universalist principles. Still, as Appleman continues, the grantmakers who come together at IF meetings "tell each other who they're funding, what exciting things are happening, and maybe suggest that there's an organization worth looking into. Thus there may well be a multiplier effect."

One of IF's primary objectives is to get people talking to each other, thereby building relationships across the chasms of race and religion by emphasizing what they have in common. What all these groups do have in common is the belief that a healthy democracy is dependent on mutual trust and shared interest among an active and involved citizenry. "A decline in participation in groups of all kinds, and an increasing isolation of individuals are weakening U.S. democracy," Appleman believes, and she points out that IF is dedicated to strengthening "third sector" organizations, like congregations and community groups, which can act to mediate the power of the public and private sectors.

In practical terms what these groups have in common is their commitment to one or more of five basic objectives: improving public schools, creating jobs, speaking up for economic justice, increasing affordable housing, and making policing more effective and accountable.

This commitment is a powerful bond—sufficiently powerful to bridge the differences that pit denominations against each other over divisive issues. As Appleman explains,

> It's unusual to have people from such differing religious traditions be able to speak with one voice on anything. Issues such as pro-life vs. pro-choice don't get in our way because there are so many things we agree on, and we don't let differences on other issues interfere with what we can do together. We all support community organizing, so that's what we work on together.

Still, sometimes there are disagreements. When some of the members, for instance, got together on a statement explaining why they opposed President Bush's faith-based initiatives, they were careful to issue it as a joint statement and not in the name of Interfaith Funders since some of their fellow members either disagreed or were prevented by their denominations from taking such public positions on the issue.

But that's an exception. There is no disagreement when it comes to IF's own funding decisions or its core activities: funding education and sponsoring collaborative research to advance the field of faith-based community organizing (FBCO).

One such research project determined in 2000 that one of the greatest challenges facing FBCOs is recruiting trained organizers. Talented staff is essential but in short supply. Talented women and minority organizers are even more difficult to recruit. In its 2001–2002 fiscal year, IF awarded five grants totaling $310,000 to five FBCO networks to support organizer recruitment.

A subsequent research project set out to study the relationship between faith-based community organizing and the congregations that support it. In asking for Veatch support for this project, IF stated as the premise that professional community organizers tell many dramatic stories of how participation in interfaith community organizing can change the internal culture of the congregation, leading to significant congregational development. But so far the findings are purely anecdotal, and through continued study IF hopes to learn how congregations whose ethical teachings lead them into this form of civic engagement can best benefit from their experiences. Once the study is complete, IF plans to convene a conference of about forty organizers, funders, clergy, and lay people to explore the role of FBCO in congregational development. As this plan indicates, the purpose of the research is not purely academic; instead it is intended as a tool for outreach, though as Appleman points out, the FBCO concept "is not as easily understood as direct service activities, such as working with soup kitchens and homeless shelters."

One way to spread the message is for community organizers to speak at religious gatherings. In 2003, the Unitarian Universalist Congregation at Shelter Rock invited Ernesto Cortés, a leader of the Industrial Areas Foundation (a Veatch grant recipient), to be the featured speaker at its annual "Veatch Sunday." He put the story in highly personal terms when he sketched this brief portrait of a typically dedicated community organization leader:

> Virginia Ramirez is one faith-based leader who underwent a transformation through her participation in the COPS (Communities Organized for Public Service) organization in San Antonio. Before her participation, Mrs. Ramirez was afraid to speak out because she felt she wasn't educated. But she was angry at the injustice in her neighborhood. . . . COPS taught Mrs. Ramirez to tap that anger and forge it into a tool for the renewal of hope in herself and her community.
>
> She learned to speak publicly, to lead actions, to take risks for herself, and to guide others. The FBCO process taught her to develop relationships within which she could challenge

the indifference and apathy of officials. She learned how to work with others to negotiate with the holders of power: to compromise, to confront when necessary, and to rebuild collaboration. She gained the confidence to lead negotiations with the city council and mayor. She went back to school at age forty-four, earned her GED, and entered college. Virginia Ramirez is now president of her parish council. She is also co-chair of COPS and represents her community at the negotiating table with the head of the chamber of commerce, the mayor, and the bankers of San Antonio [and she] mentors and guides other leaders like herself.

Multiply this story by many thousands, and the power of the community organizing movement becomes palpable. It is becoming a growing (and much needed) force to reinvigorate American democracy . . . for democratic institutions cannot thrive if they are not nourished by a dynamic civil society.

## Grassroots Institute for Fundraising Training

*Wanted:* People of color who wish to be professional fundraisers for social justice organizations. No experience required, but passionate commitment to progressive causes a must.

This want ad is made up, but the facts are real. Like community organizers, people of color with experience in raising funds are in short supply.

The Grassroots Institute for Fundraising Training (GIFT) looks for potential interns who would like to support the cause of social justice not as organizers or administrators but as the professionals who supply the lifeblood of grassroots organizations, money.

Michael Roque, GIFT's first executive director, explains why there is a need for such highly specialized professionals and why his organization is eager to recruit and train them:

When our program was first started in 1997, we looked around and saw that even among progressive organizations, even among those run by people of color, almost all the fundraisers were white. So we asked why, and we talked to the folks running these organizations and they told us that they'd love to hire a person of color, but there were no such qualified people around. So some of us started an internship program as part of another organization, and then spun off GIFT as an independent entity.

The internship program is the heart of GIFT activities. It takes on people of all ages, trains them to be professional fundraisers, and then helps to place them with a grassroots organization.

The internship lasts six months. It starts with one week of intensive orientation; then the interns go out into the field to get practical experience working for a cooperating organization. Halfway through their training, all the interns in that cycle are brought back to the Denver headquarters for a week's additional coaching, followed by three months of hands-on experience. Finally they return to headquarters for assistance with their job search: such as help preparing a résumé and making phone calls to prospective employers. In the few cases in which the candidate is not quite ready to go out on his or her own, GIFT promises the prospective employer that it will continue to do the necessary coaching.

With ten interns training at any given time, about sixty have been launched on their new careers since the inception of the program, with between 75 percent and 80 percent still working as active fundraisers. The other 20 percent are also working for nonprofit agencies, but in other capacities. Roque explains,

> There are two basic principles as to the organizations we work with. We ask: are they democratic and do they have an organized membership base of the kind of folks who are generally disenfranchised—low income, people of color, gays and lesbians—the kind of folks who traditionally have not had access to the corridors of power? Second, do they have a progressive agenda? If they want to reduce crime in their community, do they just want more cops in the neighborhood or

do they also want to make sure that there is police accountability regarding racial profiling and harassment?

The other requirement is that there be a person in charge of
fundraising the intern can work with. We prefer that there be
a development director, but we realize that a lot of smaller
social justice organizations can't afford that, but they do need
to have someone whose primary responsibility is fundraising.

Once interns are accepted into the program, they receive a
stipend of $200 a week for twenty hours of work; if necessary they
may also receive help with child care, health care, and educational
expenses. "We fly them to different locations for week-long training," Roque adds, "pay for the trainers, for the facilities, for food—
altogether it costs us about $13,000 for each intern we place."

Because of that substantial investment—the training program
amounts to some $150,000 of GIFT's total budget of about
$400,000—Roque stresses that GIFT is very cautious with its selec-
tions. "It's a big investment for us," he points out. Another reason
for being careful is that grassroots fundraising is what he calls "a
political act," just like community organizing itself. "Who raises the
money, how you raise the money, where you raise the money—all
that makes critical statements about the organization. . . . We don't
make the rules, but we do say that each organization has to ask
itself those questions."

GIFT's other activities include research to demonstrate that
philanthropy is not reserved for "rich white males" but can also be
carried on by people of color, even by low-income people. It is also
eager to demonstrate how and why grassroots organizations can
build a base of donors, particularly of donors with limited incomes.

Incidentally, Roque's successor as executive director, Sonia
Garcia, started with the organization as an intern. Not so incidentally, Veatch executive director Marjorie Fine was at one point a
member of the GIFT steering committee, demonstrating once
again that in addition to her vital role as the head of the Veatch
staff, Fine has for many years been a mover and shaker in the
entire field of progressive funding and organizing.

## The Alliance for Justice

Misconceptions about what nonprofit and tax-exempt organizations can and can't do frequently hamper the efforts of progressive nonprofit groups to be effective in the public sphere. It is the key purpose of the Alliance for Justice (AFJ) to remove these self-imposed handicaps.

In requesting continued Veatch support, the Alliance specified that it needed funding to help underwrite two of its major activities: the Nonprofit Advocacy Project and the Foundation Advocacy Initiative. These two programs, it says, "will work in tandem with the Unitarian Universalist Veatch Program, its grantees, as well as with other progressive grant-making foundations and progressive grassroots organizations throughout the country to expand social and economic justice, improve the environment, open access to the political system, and ensure that women and minorities have their full and equal civil rights."

Founded in 1979, the Alliance is made up of nearly sixty civil rights, women's, consumer, legal, environmental, and public interest organizations that help each other (and similar organizations) to participate more fully in the public policy process through training, publications, and technical support.

"These groups," says Nan Aron, AFJ executive director, "are often the only organized advocates on behalf of the *public* interest, in contrast to well-funded corporate and special interest groups."

Such nonprofit groups often feel hobbled by uncertainty about the rules that govern their lobbying and election-related activities. Even worse, the foundations funding these organizations are not sure about these rules themselves and may quite unnecessarily prohibit their grantees from engaging in permissible forms of advocacy. John Pomeranz, director of AFJ's Nonprofit Advocacy Project, sums up the problem:

> It's unfortunate that nonprofit organizations—that after all are in the front lines of addressing our most pressing social

problems—don't realize just how important they can be in the public sphere. Hopefully, our work helps to evaporate some of that misunderstanding. The good news is that just because groups tend to be overcautious, we haven't seen a lot of IRS enforcement action against charity and nonprofit organizations. There simply hasn't been any need for it. The problem is at the other end of the spectrum. They're too cautious. Far from being close to the line, they don't do nearly as much lobbying as the law permits.

Nan Aron picks up the discussion:

Compounding the problem is that organizations that are busily involved in social change simply don't have the time or the resources to fully educate themselves about IRS rules and regulations. We see our role as providing them with the information they need through workshops, books, and technical assistance, so as to equip them with a firm understanding of what they can and cannot do.

The other premise underlying our work is that lately some progressive organizations that engage in visible activism have become the target of government attacks. So our second goal is to ensure that these organizations are not chilled by fear of the government's response, but act boldly and publicly in expressing their views.

Not that concern about government threats is entirely unjustified. Aron continues,

Early in the Reagan Administration, we saw a lot of efforts to defund the left by shutting down human services programs that received government funding. Shutting down the Legal Services Corporation was one such effort. We've also seen efforts by members of Congress to investigate the behavior of charities. In the 1990s, we saw the efforts of Congressman Istook and some of his pals to put additional restrictions on advocacy by any organization that received even a dime of federal funds—even if their advocacy programs were funded by other money.

Finally, there have been attempts by independent groups, often funded by industry or fronts for industry, to silence environmental groups by accusing them of violating their tax-exempt status. Or you'll see groups working on sex education or AIDS education being challenged by outside groups. It's one more weapon your opponents can use against you—and the best defense is knowing exactly what your legal rights are.

She describes the struggle as a David and Goliath battle, with powerful forces—forces that have vastly greater resources than the nonprofit groups they attack—trying to squash the voices of democracy. With a total budget of between $4 million and $5 million, AFJ cannot redress this imbalance monetarily; what it does offer is reliable, thoroughly researched legal advice based on some fundamental facts.

Nonprofit organizations such as those supported by Veatch grants are defined by the Internal Revenue Service as public charities; they are covered by article 501(c)(3) of the Internal Revenue Code. Hence, they are often referred to as "501s" or "C3s." They are not required to pay most federal taxes, and most of the contributions they receive are tax-deductible. In return for these benefits, federal law limits their lobbying and other advocacy activities. The critical point is that these activities are limited but not outlawed, and a variety of AFJ publications detail just where the line is drawn.

In an effort to disseminate accurate information, AFJ conducts more than 125 workshops in a typical year. It also sponsors a Web site and a toll-free phone number. In fact, each year more than six hundred nonprofit organizations call this number for technical assistance in defining precisely what they can and cannot do.

"Following one of our workshops," adds Aron, "we receive dozens of requests for follow-up technical assistance and advice. While not binding legal advice, the basic information we provide saves groups hours of research and hundreds of dollars in legal fees, enabling them to concentrate more fully on carrying out their substantive agendas."

When the McCain-Feingold Campaign Finance Reform Law was passed, AFJ scored an important victory. "We were the lead agency," says Pomeranz, "in persuading the Federal Election Commission that there is no point in applying this law's advocacy provisions to charitable organizations. After all, we pointed out to them, these organizations are already so heavily regulated by the Internal Revenue Service that a second layer of regulation would be unnecessary."

As the name "*Alliance* for Justice" suggests, members share common interests and objectives, and provide each other with mutual support. The relationship between AFJ and the Veatch Program is particularly strong. Like a number of organizations, AFJ enjoys a close cooperative relationship with the Veatch staff, beyond receiving Veatch grants.

Again, Marjorie Fine is the pivotal person. Nan Aron says, "Marjorie has always thought that one of the great benefits of our work is to help the advocacy efforts of Veatch grantees. That's particularly important right now because the things that Veatch and its grantees feel most deeply about in terms of social and economic justice are currently most at risk in this country.

"Marjorie Fine is one of the few people in the philanthropic world," Aron continues, "who shares an interest in the very issues that we address here at the Alliance: the issues that deal with strengthening the voice of nonprofit organizations and foundations. So from time to time we will team up on a joint advocacy strategy."

Fine, according to Aron, has also been helpful in getting additional foundations to join AFJ, and both have been active in the National Network of Grantmakers—speaking at conferences, participating in meetings, and in every possible way spreading the word about IRS rules to their funding peers.

John Pomeranz adds, "we frequently encounter Veatch people at the events we attend. Just last week, the Center for Community Change ran a voter empowerment conference, and Bill Dempsey [at the time a Veatch program officer] attended our workshop. Afterward, I had a conversation with Bill about common issues, and that's interesting because a lot of nonprofit organizations speak to their funders only when they go to them cap in hand, whereas with Veatch it's more like an ongoing two-way conversation." Pomeranz concludes,

Occasionally we get funding from other organizations, and of course we appreciate that help, but it's not always as central to our mission as support from Veatch. What we like about Veatch is that its focus on social and economic justice and its progressive vision of society, allow us to work with groups that our hearts most lead us to. What's more, it is a personal pleasure working with them.

# Life Support for the UUA
## A Powerful Partnership Begins

AT ABOUT THE SAME time that the Veatch Program was evolving into its current professional structure and more clearly defining its twin goals of supporting the denomination and furthering its principles, the Unitarian Universalist Association (UUA) found itself in dire financial straits. When Robert West took office as the second president in 1969, he discovered that not only had all non-restricted capital been spent by the previous administration, but the association's bank held an open demand note for $450,000. On top of that, with the fiscal year already well underway, the budget was $1 million in the red. West undertook an immediate and massive reorganization that eliminated half the association's jobs and $1 million in programs. He also turned for help to the Plandome church and its Veatch resources. But, as West recalls, there was a problem. Because of the previous administration's spending practices, the Plandome congregation had zero confidence in the UUA administration:

> I spent an enormous amount of time meeting with members of the congregation and the Veatch committee, explaining my approach to the UUA's problems and attempting to regain their confidence in the UUA as a trustworthy, accountable

recipient of their grants . . . Throughout my two terms I made numerous visits to Plandome to meet with the committee, answer questions, and explain how its grants [when they finally resumed] were being spent.

Gradually a relationship of trust was rebuilt. To shore it up, West invited Eleanor Vendig to sit in on UUA board meetings as an observer. A further link was created when Robert Adelman became a member of the board as the association's financial adviser.

Soon these efforts paid off.

In 1971, the Plandome congregation agreed to lend the denomination's Beacon Press $100,000 at 6 percent interest to cover the costs of publishing the *Pentagon Papers*. Veatch funds also supported West's "Sharing in Growth" project with a grant of $98,000.

A year later, Veatch money helped the denomination find a way out of a moral as well as financial quandary. In 1968, the UUA General Assembly had voted to fund the denomination's black power–inspired Black Affairs Council (BAC) with a total of $1 million, to be paid over four years. This obligation complicated West's efforts to balance the budget and at his suggestion, the board of trustees voted to stretch the payments out over five years. This proved unacceptable to BAC and its white supporters, leading to bitter recriminations.

In an attempt to heal the wounds, the 1971 General Assembly voted to set up a Fund for Racial Justice, with money going to BAC along with other racial justice organizations such as Black and White Action (BAWA). However, efforts to implement this resolution through joint fund-raising failed to satisfy BAC, which insisted: "Not a penny for BAWA." Finally, in May 1972, the Plandome congregation voted unanimously to activate the fund with a gift of $250,000, to be supplemented with an additional $170,000 in subsequent years. (Right down to the present, the congregation has frequently supplemented denominational support with budget allocations beyond those funneled through the Veatch Program.)

## The Downside of Generosity

The fact that this sustained support was paid for out of Caroline Veatch's bequest rather than out of the members' pockets does not diminish the astonishing generosity of the congregation, which never faltered in its commitment to share its wealth with the UUA.

At the same time, the pattern of making grants in response to specific UUA requests was causing the church growing discomfort. Was it, in effect, putting a single church board in the position of passing judgment on denominational policies and programs? Could this practice lead to criticism that one congregation was being disproportionately influential?

In 1974, the Veatch board decided to convert its support of UUA into a block grant of $600,000, not only to equal its previous contributions but also to set up a special grants section to provide for new programs and services that otherwise could not be funded. Among the programs this paid for were new religious education curricula, programs on aging, and the Washington Office for Social Concern. All this was in addition to a building loan program for individual congregations and a matching gifts program for contributions to the association's annual fund. The next year, the block grant was renewed with a 3 percent increase.

Eventually the Veatch board decided to go one step further in severing what some considered a dependency relationship: it set up an endowment that would allow the UUA board to spend the fund's income as it saw fit, without waiting for the year's block grant. It was calculated that the income from this endowment, which eventually totaled $20 million, would roughly equal the Veatch funding the association had been receiving in previous years.

No wonder Robert West referred to the Veatch Program's support of the UUA as having been of "inestimable worth and benefit."

What's more, West stresses, it was not just monetary contributions that made Plandome's support so special: "It was the spirit of sharing, the sense of 'we are all in this together.'" This sentiment is echoed again and again by Veatch grant recipients, both within and outside the denomination. Veatch assistance, everyone agrees, is not just a check in the mail; it is a partnership.

Bringing West's assessment up to date, William Sinkford, the current UUA president, says, "The impact that Shelter Rock and Veatch have had on this movement has been transformative. At the broadest level, if Unitarian Universalism were to dream of a major funding source we would dream up the Shelter Rock Congregation and its Veatch Program, because their priorities are so consonant with both our values and our institutions." Then, referring to their support at times of crisis, he says, "I don't think there is any doubt that their generosity contributed significantly to the turnaround that has placed the association where it is today, so that . . . we can build on strength rather than on weakness." To put it less diplomatically, the money Caroline Veatch left to her church saved the UUA from bankruptcy at least twice.

Sinkford mentions that the yearly draw from what he calls "the Manhasset trust" is a significant part of the UUA operating budget, and singles out the support given to the Lombard/Meadville Theological School, the Starr King School for the Ministry, and the Harvard Divinity School as worthy of special praise. Among the most recent initiatives made possible by Shelter Rock and Veatch, he points to the grant to the Liberal Religious Education Association (LREDA), which has served, as he puts it, "to bring religious education out of the basement" by stimulating congregations to pay their religious educators more respectable salaries and to change "the culture around religious education."

In the 2000 fiscal year, combined Shelter Rock and Veatch funds totaled $1.9 million, accounting for 28 percent of the UUA's operating budget. That was in addition to support for Unitarian Universalist projects and organizations not under the UUA umbrella. The most significant of these grants deserve individual discussion.

## The UU Funding Program

There is something about children's voices raised in song that warms the heart and tightens the throat. This is true even when the singing is a little ragged; more so when it is as well trained as it was at the Sunday morning service of the 2003 UUA General Assembly. What the 11,000 delegates and guests in Boston's Fleet Center may not have known is that these 150 girls and boys had spent five days at a music camp rehearsing and perfecting their performance.

The inspiration for this event came from the UU Musicians Network which, having conceived of it, received a $10,000 challenge grant from the UU Funding Program (UUFP) to make it happen. "It's the kind of project we love to fund," said says Hillary Goodridge, UUFP program director. The ultimate source of the money that turns such dreams into reality is, once again, the Veatch Program. Goodridge says,

> What this Veatch funding means to the denomination is to provide an incredible resource for grassroots Unitarian Universalist projects. It enables UU congregations and organizations to grow and expand their own funding base, and provides a resource outside of the UUA budget for history, education, and ministry projects, for worship arts, and for social responsibility activities.

> Knowing that this resource exists expands people's horizons. Instead of thinking, "How would we ever pay for this?" they think, "Hey, we can do this!" And so we receive hundreds of applications. Our only requirement is that they be sponsored by an established UU congregation or organization. We can't accept requests from individuals. Then they have to meet certain standards regarding accountability and evaluation, but while it's a very serious application process, we try to make it as friendly as possible, and often we get feedback that

the questions we ask were helpful, because they made people focus on issues they might not have thought of otherwise. For instance, we ask: How are you going to structure your evaluation? What are you going to do when the grant runs out? Who are the responsible parties? Who does the work?

To review the applications, the funding program has set up four panels. Three of them deal specifically with denominational issues: the Fund for Unitarian Universalism; the Fund for International Unitarian Universalism; and the Fund for UU Social Responsibility. The fourth, the Fund for a Just Society, helps put Unitarian Universalist values into action.

Ten of the thirty-two grants from the Fund for Unitarian Universalism in 2002 were listed in the annual report under the heading of "Preserving and Disseminating our History." A renewal grant went to the First Unitarian Church of Cincinnati for its *Let Freedom Ring* project. Goodridge explains,

> This is a remarkable history project documenting the church's role in the city's underground railroad and anti-slavery movement. The congregation also researched their role in the AUA's refusal to recognize and assist an African American church founded in 1918. In 2001, members of the church and of the Northern Hills UU Fellowship held a reconciliation service to acknowledge the injustice done to the Rev. W. H. G. Carter, and to apologize to his descendants. One hundred members of the Carter family came from across the country to participate. The grandson of the Reverend Carter lit the chalice. In closing his sermon, the Rev. Mark Morrison-Reed said: "Reconciliation . . . requires truth. That is what this weekend is in part about—reconciliation. It asks that we pause to remember the history we would rather forget."

A grant to First Parish in Cambridge, Massachusetts, enabled that church to complete its online history of notable Unitarian Universalists, while the Emerson Bicentennial Committee was able to develop worship and religious education materials for local congregations eager to keep alive Ralph Waldo Emerson's contributions to American culture and his pivotal role in shaping our liberal religious tradition. Meanwhile, nearby First Parish in Brookline used its funding to prepare a television documentary on the life of Thomas Starr King intended for airing on PBS.

Grants devoted to "growing the denomination" are equally varied and imaginative. First Universalist Parish in Malden, Massachusetts, is exploring how a congregation in an urban center undergoing rapid racial, cultural, and economic changes can grow in outreach and membership. Its application noted that as urban centers experienced an exodus of well-to-do white residents starting in the 1960s, many UU congregations followed them to the suburbs. Others closed their doors. Surely, First Parish said, there must be a way to flourish in a diverse, transitional urban center, and with the help of its grant it intends to find out how to go about it.

Other grantees are exploring radio and newspaper advertising, television programs, evening forums, and outreach to particular audiences, such as individuals of Jewish background or members of the deaf community.

The list goes on. There is the $11,000 grant to the Church of the Larger Fellowship, the denomination's nonresident congregation, to create a "between Sundays" Web site, and one for $10,000 to Starr King School for the Ministry to develop courses both on-site and online for a certificate program for lay leaders.

Meanwhile the Fund for International Unitarian Universalism promotes liberal religious values in countries where there are no local sources of such support.

Rev. Mark Allstrom was minister of the Unitarian Church in Adelaide when it received a $7,500 grant for a radio program, "to make Australians aware that there is a liberal religious alternative to the conservative and fundamentalist churches on which many of them have turned their backs." Allstrom explains how this came about:

The minister of our church in Sidney was interviewed on a national radio station, and we got phone calls from all over the country from people who wanted to know whether there was a Unitarian church near them. That made us realize how potent radio could be in Australia, where distances are so vast, and we found that we could have a half-hour weekly show in Adelaide for only about $24 U.S. Then we got the idea that we could tape these shows and send them off to other cities for rebroadcast, but that took money we didn't have. So we asked whether the UU International Funding Panel might entertain an application from Australia.

We received a grant that allows us to bounce our program off a satellite that then beams it to radio stations all over the country. The show is about the interface of religion and culture . . . not specifically about Unitarianism, but it is identified as coming from the Unitarian Church of South Australia and that it is supported by the UU Funding Panel.

So far there have been more than a hundred such programs. With some revisions and reedits they are also being used in New Zealand, and there is a possibility that they may be adapted for Unitarian congregations in the Khasi Hills of India, possibly even in the Fiji Islands. Says Allstrom, "Without the UUFP money we wouldn't have been able to go national or even to continue with the program."

Like many such efforts, the radio programs have had a ripple effect, and this time the ripple did not have to travel far. Mark Allstrom's wife, Louise, was project coordinator of a church program called "Unitarians for Refugees." It started off trying to help Afghans who had fled from the Taliban, made their way from Pakistan to Indonesia, then were smuggled to Australia, many of them winding up in Adelaide. "Unitarians for Refugees" decided to find out how they could help. As Louise Allstrom explains,

We quickly realized that we couldn't give them all the help they needed, so we decided to concentrate on what we could do best. I met with a man called Mohammed Amkar, a horticulturist who had worked for the government until the Taliban put him in jail. As an educated man he spoke pretty good English and so he became an adviser to us and we realized that the first priority had to be to help these men, and they were almost all men, to learn English. Some didn't know how to read and write even in their own language; others were well educated but didn't know English, and without it there was no way to earn money, both to support themselves and, once the Taliban fell, to send some home.

Because their needs were so different, we taught them one-on-one. We also tried to give them furniture and kitchen equipment and help them make a living, but most important, we tried to create a community, a supportive network, and to enable them to become permanent residents so that they could bring their families to Australia.

Having financed their program mostly through fund-raising dinners, the volunteers found it a big help when, inspired by Allstrom's grant, they applied for and received matching grants of $2,000 the first year and $1,000 the second from the UU Funding Program. The grants not only put them on a firmer financial basis but enabled them to add new programs. Now they were able to offer a bus trip to the beach for recreation and goodwill. On the way back, the Afghans spontaneously began to sing songs in their own languages. "By this time they had learned to trust us enough to be able to relax. We've come a long way," Louise sums up. One man even showed her a picture of his wife—something in violation of strict Islamic rules.

The wide range of applications that the funding program encourages also presents a problem. As Goodridge explains, "how do you pit a history project against a worship arts project against a social responsibility project? It's like trying to decide between apples and oranges." That was the reason for setting up four different funding panels and giving each an allocation from the total Veatch grant, so that every proposal would be reviewed in comparison with others in its category. Because all panels use as their parameters the basic Veatch criteria, it is no surprise that a number of UU Funding Panel grants go to organizations that also receive direct support from Veatch or from the Shelter Rock congregation. Thus Starr King School, in addition to its UUFP grant, has also received gifts for financial aid to students from allocations by the congregation beyond the Veatch budget.

Here are other examples of the way the stream of Veatch money finds its way in mutually supportive rivulets to achieve common objectives:

- When the UU Congregation of Miami wanted to help the South Florida Interfaith Committee for Worker Justice, a Veatch grantee, it received a $2,000 grant from the Fund for Social Responsibility that enabled it to co-sponsor the volunteer training program.

- When All Souls UU Church of Kansas City, Missouri, wanted to help launch an interfaith program to promote racial justice and cross-cultural understanding, a three-year challenge grant helped it to get the Congregational Partners Program up and running.

- Beacon Press received a UUFP grant to enable it to establish an internship program for people of color.

Both ACORN (Association of Community Organizations for Reform Now) and Jobs with Justice chapters have received support from local congregations that in turn received grants from the Fund for a Just Society. The dual objective is to help grassroots organizations, while also stimulating involvement in social justice projects by UU congregations and individuals.

Another priority of the social justice fund is to support issues and positions that have won backing at General Assemblies, in particular the Statements of Conscience that set denominational priorities.

Whenever a social justice grant is approved, an announcement goes to nearby UU congregations. Another way the grants panels seek to generate a multiplier effect is to make a growing number of challenge grants, requiring the recipients to do their own fund-raising within the next thirteen months. In about 80 percent of cases this condition is met, and over the past three years, eighty-three of the social responsibility and just society grants have been challenge grants, as have fifty-five of the domestic and international denominational grants. The Funding Program's report to Veatch for 2003 to 2004 points out that if all of these challenges are met, they will produce close to $500,000 in new money for the denomination and its causes, a fair return in monetary terms alone on the Veatch investment.

Despite a firm policy against funding anything commercial, the UU Funding Program recently made an exception. The Unitarian Universalist Church of the Philippines, serving a largely poor community, has few sources of income. They came up with the idea that if they could start a mango plantation on church property it would generate enough income to make them self-sufficient. "We had to do a lot of research to make this decision," Goodridge recalls, "and found out that it takes three to seven years for your first mango crop. First, you plant peanuts and bananas, which grow quickly; then you wait. Given the circumstances, their plan made sense, and so we provided the money to get them started." After the first year, the panel voted a second grant of $12,900. "It is humbling," Goodridge sums up, "to see how much a relatively small grant can create."

## Refueling Beacon Press

For ninety years, starting in 1902, Beacon Press used as its logo a stylized version of the beacon that once stood at the top of Beacon Hill. Here is how Susan Wilson explains the choice in her history of the press's first 150 years:

> Though the name Beacon had been occasionally used on earlier hymnals and prayer books, a new moniker was deemed essential for the broadened, twentieth-century identity of the publishing house. The "Beacon" referred to Beacon Hill,

where the AUA had established its permanent home. But it specifically made reference to the object that had given Beacon Hill its name nearly three centuries earlier.

In 1634, when Beacon Hill was sixty feet taller, a tar bucket was suspended from a pole on its top. If colonial Boston needed to be warned of enemies approaching by land or by sea, the bucket was set aflame and hoisted up the pole. The idea of shedding light to warn of imminent danger was appealing to the American Unitarian Association, and it was adopted for the original Beacon colophon design.

The only problem is that the metaphorical beacon bucket has from time to time run low on fuel. As a small, independent publishing house, Beacon Press chooses its titles not for their commercial potential, but either to be of service to the association's member congregations and their individual members or, as a recent slogan put it, as the denomination's "voice for good in the world." Once in a while it nonetheless comes up with a best seller (a best seller in Beacon Press terms being any title that tops ten thousand copies), which helps to make up for the many titles that barely break even. In flat years, Beacon has had to be subsidized by the UUA, and when the association is itself having budget problems, the very existence of the press is sometimes at stake. Twice in recent years there has been talk of selling it. Once a board decision to do so was reversed by the UUA General Assembly. Most recently, in 2002, the press was put on notice that if it could not control its deficits, it would have to make drastic cuts in expenses.

"It was a very tough time," says Helene Atwan, Beacon's director. "We looked around and wondered what more we could cut. There was nothing left to cut except staff—a very grim scenario." Laying off people would have meant publishing fewer books, thus further reducing income and entering into a downward spiral that might be difficult to reverse. At that point, according to Atwan, the Veatch Program approved a grant of $75,000. "The operational support grant from Veatch enabled us to balance our budget without cutting staff," Atwan explains. "It meant that we were able to close in the black, and we are deeply grateful, especially as the grant was renewed for the next fiscal year."

Nor was this the first time Veatch or Shelter Rock money had saved Beacon from sputtering into darkness. The first crisis occurred when the publication of the *Pentagon Papers* helped preserve First Amendment rights—but at the risk of bankrupting the UUA and of sending its president to jail.

When the nation was being torn apart by the Vietnam War, the Nixon Administration used every possible means, both legal and illegal, to suppress dissent. The Defense Department had launched an internal review—what was to become known as the "Pentagon Papers"—of the decisions that led the country into war. Daniel Ellsberg, a Pentagon official, decided that the lies and cover-ups these papers documented should be made public, and he leaked copies to the *Washington Post* and the *New York Times*. But the newspapers published only excerpts. To make the full record available for libraries and scholars, Senator Mike Gravel of Alaska, a Unitarian Universalist and committed critic of the war, agreed to try to find a publisher. In a nighttime parking lot encounter worthy of a spy thriller, he was given a copy of the report, but every publisher he queried turned him down.

Finally Gravel turned to his own denomination, and Beacon Press agreed to publish the four-volume edition despite the enormous cost and risk. The government had already taken the *Post* and *Times* to court and Nixon, determined to find the leak, had authorized his "plumbers" to break in to the Democratic Watergate offices.

White House retribution was not long in coming. Gobin Stair, then director of the press, received a personal phone call from President Nixon; FBI agents rummaged through the UUA's bank records seeking the names of members and contributors; and a grand jury contemplated criminal charges—all triggering tremendous legal costs on top of the publishing expense.

It took court action to stop the FBI. It took a Veatch loan to save Beacon Press and the UUA from financial ruin. Then, in 1975, Beacon Press received a $300,000 loan for operating capital.

When no repayments had been made by 1985, the loan was converted into a grant.

In the early 1990s Veatch helped out again, giving Beacon yearly grants of $100,000 for three years for the acquisition of books that Wendy Strothman, the director at the time, deemed critical to fulfill the Beacon mission. As it happened, one of the manuscripts acquired was Marion Wright Edelman's *The Measure of Our Success*, one of Beacon's trail-blazing books on African American issues. "That was so wildly successful," says Atwan, "that Wendy didn't need the money for the second and third years."

Atwan herself turned to Veatch, not for general support but to underwrite a program to build greater awareness of Beacon among Unitarian Universalists. She says,

> Together with Marjorie Fine of the Veatch Program I developed the idea that we should publish reading guides specifically for Unitarian Universalist congregations. In addition, we needed to expand our Web site to include resources to help congregations use Beacon books in their congregational work.
>
> That was the beginning of the whole concept of a UU outreach program that we developed over the next two years. It struck me that here was this tremendous denominational resource, but many Unitarian Universalists didn't even seem aware of it. Even now, only about four or five percent of our sales are through UU channels, though individual UUs whom we can't identify may be buying our books through Amazon or Barnes & Noble. Anyway, we received a Veatch grant that permitted us to hire an outreach coordinator whose job was to go to district and regional meetings and to develop workshops at General Assembly featuring Beacon books and authors.
>
> Person-by-person and minister-by-minister we were able to reach out to UU congregations and make them aware of Beacon books not only for individual readers but as resources in congregational life. And just this year, we received an

additional "mini-grant" of $4,500 for a 150th anniversary catalog of books specifically for UUs. Unlike our general catalogues, it uses the UUA principles as its categories, so that, for example, it's easy to find books that promote the inherent worth and dignity of every person, or those that encourage spiritual growth.

Additional Veatch money flowed to the press through a grant from the UU Funding Panel that underwrote Beacon's internships for people of color. "The lack of diversity is a real problem for the publishing industry," Atwan points out. "For three years, this wonderful program allowed us to bring quite a few of our graduates into the industry."

Veatch help has been invaluable, she concludes:

The publishing world is a tough place, especially now that the economy is bad and the media are consumed by trivia. If we have been able to persist and thrive it's in large measure thanks to the support—not just money, but concepts and encouragement—that we've received from Veatch.

## The UU Service Committee

To an astonishing degree, given the diversity of its grants, Veatch has become a partner of the organizations it supports, not interfering or attempting to give direction, but identifying the essence of the recipients' objectives and offering insights into ways to maximize them. Of no organization is that more true than the Unitarian Universalist Service Committee (UUSC).

As far back as 1979, Ed Lawrence, director of what was then the Veatch committee, became concerned that funding individual UUSC programs could become tantamount to interference. "While it's one thing," he said, "to go ahead and fund one program, when you begin to fund three or four and you say, 'No, I don't like that program, I like this one,' you're beginning to impose your own judgment as to the nature of the organization that is your grantee." Veatch therefore bowed out of the decision-making process, instead offering to match Service Committee contributions, at first dollar for dollar, and later based on varying formulas. Currently, Veatch matches all contributions of more than $60 up to a maximum of $675 each. This decision, of course, parallels the intent of, but does not duplicate, the switch Veatch made in its support of the Unitarian Universalist Association.

And partnership is a two-way street. Back in the earliest days of the Veatch Program, the Service Committee's bail-bond project inspired a similar Veatch-funded program in Nassau County.

The Veatch/UUSC partnership reflects the fact that they share parallel objectives. As the Service Committee's mission statement says, it too is "grounded in Unitarian Universalist principles that affirm the worth, dignity, and human rights of every person, and the interdependence of all life," going on to describe itself as, "a voluntary, nonsectarian organization working to advance justice throughout the world."

The (then Unitarian) Service Committee was founded during World War II to save the lives of refugees from Nazism, and for more than sixty years it has sought to help victims of injustice both at home and around the world. While sometimes, when the need is acute, as in the aftermath of the attack on the World Trade Center, it carries out direct relief efforts, its emphasis is on bringing about lasting social change by forming partnerships with grassroots organizations so that the impact of its work carries on even after its contributions end. Thus it seeks out human rights organizations worldwide that have a strong mission, sound leadership, and above all, local support in their own communities. In the words of Charlie Clements when he assumed the presidency in 2003, "the UU Service Committee has been part of a revolution of hope and resistance since its creation." Referring to what he calls the Unitarian Universalist tradition of justice-making, he describes his vision for the Service Committee as, "saying no to fear" and "standing firm in our efforts to affirm the dignity and worth of every person."

Lately, the committee's major areas of emphasis have been to protect the rights of women and children and to advocate for the rights of oppressed, indigenous peoples in Africa, Central America, Asia, and the Caribbean. Domestically, UUSC runs work camps for adolescents, sponsors a "Welfare Rights Monitoring Project," and organizes site visits to centers of oppression for members of Congress to let them see firsthand the human rights impact of U.S. policies. Among its most recent initiatives are a "Defending Democracy" project to encourage maximum participation in the electoral process and an ambitious effort to "Stop Torture Permanently."

Part of the Service Committee's effectiveness comes from the fact that it seeks to mobilize its 32,000 members and supporters not only to give money but also to help change the policies that create unjust situations in the first place. Playing off the old saw that a relief agency gives people fish to eat whereas a development agency teaches people to fish, the UUSC, in the words of former staff member Bill Docker, tries to "make sure that the path to the fishing hole is open and protected so that everyone has access."

In support of these objectives, Veatch contributions to the Service Committee have been sizable for several decades. In 1974 it supported the general fund as well as specific projects (like criminal justice and help for Haiti) with grants totaling $185,000; the next year the total came to $225,000. The total UUSC budget was then about $600,000, so these grants made a real difference. In later years, the emphasis of the Veatch support shifted to incentive grants to encourage support by UU individuals and congregations.

In line with its view of itself as a partner, not just a source of money, Veatch has repeatedly played a significant role in enhancing UUSC's overall effectiveness, most recently with designated grants in the 1990s.

Denise Moorehead, the Service Committee's director for communications, says these grants have functioned like venture capital by providing seed money to start new programs or to move existing programs in new directions. She explains,

For instance, they have permitted us to better encourage UU congregations to become more involved in our social justice programs. We have also received direct support along the same lines from the Shelter Rock Congregation, and in the early nineties they funded a study of our internal structure that led to the appointment of a chief operating officer to free the executive director from some of the administrative details. After a couple of years, this position was absorbed into our regular operating fund—a perfect example of seed money.

Other examples include a grant of $100,000 per year for three years to develop the work camp program, a one-year grant to track the problems caused by welfare reform, and two years of funding to send delegates to the World Conference Against Racism.

"Veatch money," Moorehead continues, "has allowed us to create programs that resonate with congregations so that—either as entities or through their individual members—they will work with us on social justice issues. It has enabled us to bridge the work of our partners working for oppressed communities both overseas and in this country with the congregations." In the year when arson destroyed a number of African American churches, for example, Unitarian Universalist teenagers were recruited to help rebuild them. Such building of links and bridges is one of the continuing strategies UUSC pursues in its effort to boost its effectiveness, to help its partner organizations, and to foster the involvement of the entire denomination in the achievement of its goals. Having relatively limited resources, Moorehead sums up, UUSC is forever looking for ways to make two plus two equal five.

Sometimes, by being closely in touch with Service Committee activities but not part of the structure, Veatch is able to fill the role of a friendly but critical observer. Again, Moorehead sheds light on how this works:

Over the years, Veatch has challenged us when they felt that we were not conceptualizing programs fully, to make sure that the UU movement was involved in a hands-on way, and in general to help us be more effective in our work. The latest example, in 2002, was their funding of a capacity assessment by a consulting company to look critically at where we had room to grow. That study triggered a lot of thinking internally that proved to be very useful. It also led to our reaching out to all of our constituencies, our members and our partners, as well as the UUA, to find out where they would like to see us go. Their conclusions served as a blueprint for the new president and program director, as well as for the board of trustees. All told, their support has been fabulous!

This sentiment aptly reflects the consensus of Veatch Program grant recipients, not only those that are part of our denominational family, but the progressive, mostly grassroots organizations that, in their struggle for social justice, reflect and implement Unitarian Universalist principles.

# Omaha Together One Community
## *Fighting for Workers' Rights*

ON TUESDAY, APRIL 8, 2003, American Airlines flight 2085 lifted off from New York's LaGuardia airport. On board were two staff members and two members of the board of governors of the Veatch Program on their way to Omaha, Nebraska. According to Victor Quintana, senior program officer, site visits supplement the steady contact by phone and e-mail that Veatch program officers maintain with grant recipients, and annual field trips such as this are carefully planned to minimize expenses by going to geographically clustered locations. After landing in Omaha, the Veatch delegation piled into a rented van and went to visit grant recipients in Nebraska, Iowa, and Missouri, meeting with a total of six different organizations. Board members participate in these trips to give them—representing the decision makers who approve the grants—an opportunity to answer the question that members of the Shelter Rock congregation ask from time to time: *What happens to our money?* In addition to Quintana, the group consisted of Veatch executive director Marjorie Fine; board members Masamichi Itoh, Zed Kesner, and Jill Hyer; and one observer, the author of this book.

Geography, however, was not the only strand that the organizations included in the itinerary. As Marjorie Fine pointed out, they also illustrate many of the major program areas that the Veatch Program is currently emphasizing: immigrant and worker rights; grassroots democracy projects; environmental protection; family farms; and Unitarian Universalist social action. In addition to supervising the program officers and support staff, Fine takes direct responsibility for denominational grants and progressive philanthropy. And, of course, a major part of her job is to be the liaison between the staff and the Veatch board of governors.

An intangible benefit for the six people who traveled some thousand miles to meet dozens of people who are, in turn, changing the lives of thousands more is this: the satisfaction of observing firsthand what, together, the Veatch Program and its grantees are able to achieve. To share that satisfaction with the wider audience of readers is a primary objective of this book.

Victor Quintana, in planning the 2003 trip, had arranged with each of the called-on organizations to put together a panel of staff members, volunteer leaders, and representative beneficiaries. Together they would tell not only the organizational story but add their personal perspectives.

The first stop on the tour was at the headquarters of Omaha Together One Community (OTOC). It had just moved into a newly refurbished building, and the office, quite unlike those of most nonprofit organizations, was freshly painted, brightly lit, and—as yet—uncluttered. As with all of the encounters, this meeting began with a round of introductions, starting with Victor, who was careful to pronounce his name "Kintana" to reflect his Puerto Rican heritage. Marjorie Fine used the opportunity to explain some basic facts about the Veatch Program, saying: "Veatch is not an acronym. It is the name of a woman, Caroline Veatch, whose generous bequest to a Unitarian Universalist congregation made the Veatch Program possible." Then she briefly sketched the story of how an initially modest income had turned into a fortune:

> The Unitarian Universalist Congregation at Shelter Rock decided to put the money to use for a twofold objective: to strengthen the denomination of which it is a part, and to

further its underlying principles, which stress social justice, the democratic process, and respect for the environment. In pursuit of these objectives, it set up the UU Veatch Program, and each year the congregation votes to support the program as generously as it can. This year [2003], that total is $10.5 million, but the depletion of the German gas wells and the state of the economy may make it impossible to equal that in future years.

Tom Holler, OTOC's original organizer and director, then introduced the members of the panel. Sitting on the panel were two staff members, Sergio Sosa and Marcella Cervantes, members of the Omaha Joint Union Organizing Committee, who explained the effort to organize the "kill floor" workers of the local meat-packing plants. Because the workforce is primarily Latino, most of the panelists spoke Spanish (with a translator), although the workforce also includes Vietnamese, Afghan, and Bosnian immigrants. The employers hire anyone willing to work in deplorable conditions at minimum wage and not "make trouble." It was precisely the *need* to make trouble—that is, to ask for basic rights—that led to OTOC's initiative.

Slim, trim, and dressed like a business executive on a casual Friday, Holler explained how the experience of the latest wave of immigrants follows a pattern established in the nineteenth century. In those days, unskilled employees were largely Czechs, Poles, and Italians, but while they too were exploited, conditions in the original stockyards and packing houses were not as foul and dangerous then as they are now. In those days, quarters of slaughtered animals were shipped to local markets, where butchers cut them up for retail sale. Now production-line butchering concentrates on the preparation of "boxed beef," with each worker making one prescribed cut as each carcass whizzes by—the same cut over and over and over, all day long, day after day. At the end of the "disassembly line," each product—whether chucks, ribs, or loins—is ready for the ultimate consumer. Anyone who has read *Fast Food Nation* by Eric Schlosser has a pretty good idea of what this means for the workers, but even Schlosser's hair-raising descriptions do not have the impact of the workers' personal stories which the Veatch delegation heard that day.

The OTOC panel explained how poverty and terror had driven them to Omaha and how their experiences there had turned them into activists. Sergio Sosa, for instance, had been organizing poor peasants in Guatemala until his father was killed and he himself had to flee for his life. His conscience, he explains, was aroused by the injustices he saw every day at home, and seeing more when he arrived in Omaha. "Seeing dead, dead, and more dead, all this begins to create something inside that enrages you and makes you want to do something," he continues. And so he was happy to be hired by Holler to work for OTOC.

Holler himself had come to Omaha in 1992 by way of Detroit and San Antonio as an Industrial Areas Foundation (IAF) organizer. This organization was inspired by Saul Alinsky who, while helping workers in the Chicago stockyards get unionized in the 1930s and 1940s, developed techniques of community organization that can be summed up in the slogan that still introduces an OTOC brochure, "*Democracy is not a spectator sport.*" Today there are some fifty organizations in the IAF network, several supported by Veatch grants. Now Holler is in charge of a three-state region for IAF, all of them seriously affected by the restructuring of the meat-packing industry. Here is his explanation of how it happened:

> By the 1970s, new methods of production enabled a small group of independent producers to challenge the heavily unionized industry. Improvements in highway transport and refrigerated trucks allowed companies to move plants into rural areas. Iowa Beef Packing (IBP) showed the way. They introduced boxed beef and also recruited nonunion immigrant labor from Los Angeles, south Texas, and Mexico. They sent out recruiters and ran TV ads promising high wages and good benefits, and brought busloads of hopeful applicants to small towns in Nebraska, Kansas, and Missouri.

Faced with this competition, the old-line packing house operations sold out to faceless corporate giants like IBP, ConAgra, and Cargill, who by the 1970s and 80s dominated the meat-packing industry. Often unable to speak English, the nonunionized workers were easily intimidated, especially if they were undocumented aliens. Not only could they be fired if they complained, but the employers conspired with INS [Immigration and Naturalization Service] to stage raids and deport those who were part of any organizing effort. By 1999, hourly wages had dropped to where they had been twenty years before.

What unions were left often made sweetheart deals with the employers, and when economic factors alone did not suffice to convert the industry into lawless fiefdoms, gang-related "consultants" provided additional persuasion. By 1997, things in Omaha had got so bad that members of Our Lady of Guadalupe parish met informally to compare notes about their working conditions. Their list of concerns included brutal line speed-ups; repetitive motion injuries; cheating on wages because of lack of time clocks; unjust terminations after injuries; even lack of adequate bathroom breaks, forcing workers to urinate on the job.

The overall result was a return to "the jungle" described so vividly by Upton Sinclair in his 1906 book of that name. Ironically, the conditions Sinclair described did not end until Alinksy helped workers to organize the now-defunct United Meat Packers Union, and now, at the start of the twenty-first century, Alinksy's strategies are needed once again. Also mirroring the antilabor attitude of governments a hundred years ago, the Bush Administration repealed workplace ergonomic standards and stacked the National Labor Relations Board (NLRB) and its regional directors with anti-union appointees.

In a lunchtime tour of the city, Holler pointed out abandoned stockyards and vast stretches where traditional packing houses had been torn down. "What's needed," he said, "is to create Latino solidarity, so they don't cross picket lines and perceive their common interest. That's why, unlike the unions, which focus on specific issues, OTOC emphasizes creating community coalitions. When you're organizing in a plant, you're organizing on the employers' turf, but when you organize in the community, you're organizing on *your* turf."

After the break, a second panel took over to present firsthand reports on how community organization works, featuring Paul Turner, OTOC's lead organizer; Father Damian Zuerlein of the parish of Our Lady of Guadalupe; and Marco Nuñez, a union organizer. Father Damian, bearded and balding, exuded gentleness, but when he spoke, he appeared a lot tougher than he looked:

> I came to my parish in 1990, and when I heard from my parishioners about the conditions they were subjected to, I thought naively that if I called these problems to the attention of management they would do something about it. So I called on the head of one company, but instead of thanking me he got very angry. In fact, they did then build some more women's bathrooms, but refused to do anything else.

That lesson in civic virtue led Father Damian to become one of the founders of OTOC. Now his parish is one of several Catholic parishes that make up the organization, along with Baptist, Lutheran, Presbyterian, Methodist, Jewish, and Unitarian Universalist congregations, as well as some civic organizations. In fact, to make the Veatch delegation feel at home during this visit, Cheri Cody, representing one of the two UU member groups, met them at the door with a cheery "You're in the right place. I knew it had to be you when a van pulled up!"

The conditions that had upset Father Damian were graphically described by one woman who demonstrated how, as each piece of beef sweeps past on an overhead chain, she has to grab hold of it with a metal hook in her left hand, then perform a quick carving operation with a razor-sharp knife in her right—over and over and over. Between cuts, she has to sharpen her knife, and if she drops it, she has to pick it up while the meat keeps coming. Of course that means she does not have time to wash it, since the line never slows down. In fact, far from ever slowing down, the line is periodically speeded up to increase productivity—resulting in more accidents and in more painful and disabling repetitive motion injuries. One man experienced so much pain that he couldn't even open a door. And anyone who can no longer work receives no health benefits and is only rarely reassigned to a less stressful job. If you complain, you're fired.

## The Power of Solidarity

Gradually, word about OTOC and the unions spread, and in one plant the workers managed to collect enough petition signatures to force a National Labor Relations Board (NLRB) election. The company bused in workers from other plants and the union lost, but a second election finally led to union recognition. However, since Nebraska is a "Right to Work" state, Nuñez pointed out, a closed shop is forbidden, and the struggle to sign up new hires despite the constant threats and intimidation never ends. He said that there are three things he has learned in his two-and-a-half years as an OTOC organizer:

> The first is that conditions in these meat-packing plants are every bit as bad as has been reported. I remember one woman with such a bad case of motion injury that she couldn't hold her newborn baby. Second, the rules are not fair. The U.S. Department of Labor and the NLRB are not about to help the workers, no matter how bad the conditions. And third, labor unions can't do it alone. We would need to go plant to plant, educating and motivating workers, and the employers would pit one group against another. That's why we lost the first election. Third, if you stick together you can win.

The Sunday before the second election, Father Damian held a special mass at which he introduced Olga Espinoza, who works on the kill floor and is a member of the union's organizing committee.

She asked everyone in favor of the union to stand. Only a couple of dozen people dared to do so. She was disappointed but not defeated. At the end of the mass she asked everyone who worked at the plant to come forward to receive Father Damian's blessing. Slowly, a few men and women shuffled forward, but after a few moments, more than a hundred workers were on their feet. That turned the tide.

"We knew if we could stand up in church on Sunday, we could do it in the plant on Monday," Espinoza said later. What OTOC has done is to bridge the gap between union and community. And it not only helped win elections but now it keeps the union accountable and sensitive to the members' needs.

That experience and other OTOC activities, such as its Latino Soccer League, have succeeded in building a sense of solidarity that offers hope for a better future. It is, as Victor Quintana pointed out in recommending a $35,000 grant for OTOC, a basic Veatch and IAF strategy, the so-called Iron Rule: *Never do for those you are trying to help what they can do themselves.* It is a strategy that the United Food and Commercial Workers failed to apply in the first campaign to unionize the ConAgra plant, but had, as he explained, learned by the second:

> In the initial campaign, union organizers distributed flyers in front of the plant, ran committee meetings, and union attorneys conducted workshops. The meetings were efficiently conducted and the issues discussed important. But there was a glaring problem: The workers were not asked to participate in these leadership activities, so they did not learn how to run meetings, speak publicly, or inspire one another.

> OTOC attributes its eventual victory at ConAgra to applying the Iron Rule. Workers planned and ran their meetings, organized their own plant newsletter, planned and executed community events, challenged management, gained confidence, and won recognition on election day.

Their reward was a contract that included a 65-cent hourly raise; placing monitors at workstations to prevent production line speed-ups; and job guarantees when workers have to take time off to deal with immigration issues. A secondary benefit was a new sense of optimism that spread to workers in other plants, particularly through OTOC-sponsored house meetings. "The world of low-wage employment," in Tom Holler's words, "is one of command and control. It is a place where humiliation of workers becomes routine." So even if the new sense of solidarity was slow in forging improvements in working conditions, it paid off quickly in the workers' new-found sense of self-confidence and self-respect.

When a ConAgra vice president addressed a mandatory meeting at the plant before the second election, issuing vague promises and not-so-subtle threats—a tactic that had worked the first time—the workers started hooting and yelling. After the vice president finished, Espinoza pushed her way to the microphone and demanded, "If you're so concerned about us, why haven't you fixed the place where Tiberio fell and was hurt? Are you waiting for someone else to get hurt?" (Instead, Tiberio was fired.) When a company officer said she would answer that question if someone came to her office later, the workers began chanting, "Now! Now!" Espinoza recalls, "Then they told us there wasn't any more time for questions and to go back to work. We just hooted them down."

The vote to organize clinched the victory. But the victory had already been won in the personal transformations that gave the workers the courage to hoot . . . given them the understanding that one person who hoots can be fired, but that when everybody hoots, they're hard to stop.

# Iowa Citizens for Community Improvement
## *Saving the Family Farm and the Urban Community*

From Omaha the Veatch van traveled to Des Moines for a meeting with Iowa Citizens for Community Improvement (CCI). The "hogs" that the CCI deals with come in two varieties: the animals being raised by Iowa family farmers, and the exploiters who are threatening their farms and livelihoods—and the state's environment—by establishing hog factories where thousands of animals are penned under inhumane conditions.

The $35,000 grant CCI received from the Veatch Program for 2003 was for organizing "rural and urban communities to challenge factory farming in the livestock industry." The CCI had established its credibility the year before (with the help of a similar grant) by exposing the fact that the head of the state Senate's Natural Resources Committee was a full-time employee of a major hog factory corporation, a scandal that led him not to seek reelection. It was, however, only one of the threats facing family farmers, not only in Iowa but in all hog-breeding states.

The posters in the room where Larry Ginter, a farmer and key CCI leader, assembled his expert panel told the story of the struggle even before the dialogue began: "Reclaiming our neighborhoods ... reclaiming our farms ... reclaiming democracy," "Family farms yes! Factory farms no!" "Stand up. Speak out. Fight back."

Ginter explained that CCI became active in the early 1980s when a farm depression triggered numerous bankruptcies and foreclosures: "Then there was a new crisis in the 90s, with the corporate takeover of family farms. We organized a lot of people—we now have 1,800 members—and we speak out and fight back."

The presenters he introduced included a mix of farm people and city residents, representing various ethnic and occupational groups. They all had one thing in common: the determination to fight for justice that had inspired them to form an unusual rural-urban coalition. Ron Brada presented the farmers' point of view: "Factory farms are ruining everything on our land. They're very good at it, so we have to learn to be even better at fighting them." Phil Dabner, another long-term member, spoke from the perspective of a city resident: "CCI has enabled me to fulfill some of the dreams I had about being a citizen of Des Moines. I'm most grateful for their help."

In 1900, when one out of every ten Americans made their living in farming, "family farms" would have been a tautology. There was no other kind. Today, when fewer than one in one hundred make their living farming, the retrofit term "family farmers" has become necessary to distinguish them from the corporate owners who have turned farming into an industry.

Rosie Partridge, another CCI member, explained how hard it has been to fight the spread of factory farms because it is so difficult to organize opposition in rural areas. Families are fairly isolated, she said, so it's not like going door-to-door or even block by block. Also, farmers have a strong tradition of self-sufficiency and are reluctant to ask for help. "But we knew," Partridge said, "that if we didn't organize to stop factory farms we'd lose everything. And CCI taught us how."

CCI has also helped farmers win some victories. "Hog confinement stopped near Dexter," read the headline in the *Iowa Dallas County News* on October 17, 2002. "7,000-head sow factory construction halted."

"We live 2,100 feet from the site and we didn't want this operation so near to our farm," the news story goes on to quote Barb Kalbach, a farmer who along with her husband Jim belongs to CCI. "We made history with this vote." They were joined in their protest by more than three thousand other residents who signed a petition opposing the proposed facility. Hugh Espey, CCI rural projects director, explained why neighbors fight so hard (but not always so successfully) to keep factory farms from moving into their area. Their air, water, health, and quality of life, not to mention property values, are all at stake:

> The hogs stand on slats and their feces and urine—what doesn't cling to the slats—drop into concrete pits below the building. When the pits are pumped out, there are millions and millions of gallons of manure that are spread on the ground, and from there some of it drains into streams and gets into the groundwater.

In addition, emissions of toxic fumes, particularly hydrogen sulfide and ammonia, poison the air for miles around, causing both neurological and pulmonary complications. The response of the Bush Administration's Environmental Protection Agency to these complaints, incidentally, has been a proposal to exempt factory farms from the provisions of the Clean Air Act—in the name of research. One prong of CCI's antifactory farm battle is on the legislative front. Campaign finance reform is a basic issue. In the last race for governor, the CEO of Iowa Select, which owns 100,000 sows, gave one candidate $44,000 and his wife gave an additional $50,000. The head of Heartland Pork (61,000 sows) ponied up $35,000 for the Republican party and $6,000 for the Democrats.

In Washington, Iowa CCI is backing legislation to ban packer ownership of livestock. The state already has a similar law, but it is being challenged in the courts by a packer called Smithfield. Borrowing a leaf from the book of their more militant urban brethren, the farmers marched to the home of a local Smithfield official, carrying placards and leaving a round-robin letter at his door. Other items on the CCI legislative agenda are to strip the proindustry Department of Natural Resources of its power to control their sites and turn the siting decisions over to local counties; to establish enforceable air quality standards; and to declare a moratorium on construction or expansion of factory farms with more than twenty-five hundred hogs at any one time. All these goals were summed up on CCI's 2003 legislative rally day, with CCI members carrying signs that said, "Stop Polluting our Environment/Stop Polluting Our Democracy," and "It's Time to Fight Corporate Concentration."

To add a human dimension to this struggle, the visitors next heard from Rosie Partridge, Garry Klicker, and Nadine Mortensen. Partridge joined in 1995 at a rally that featured Farm Aid president and cofounder Willie Nelson, the populist country singer. The rally launched the Campaign for Family Farms, of which CCI is a member. What mobilized Partridge was the arrival of the first industrial hog farm in her county. "They come to the communities and tear them apart," she says. "They bring nothing, and drive people away." And as the family farmers give up and move away, they leave behind additional land where the industrial farms can spread their blight. Speaking of the importance of Veatch support, Partridge particularly praised the matching funds to stimulate the individual fund-raising campaign CCI had launched. "It's a real incentive," she said.

Klicker, wearing a "Stop Factory Farms" T-shirt, added, "it's an assault on our communities, our schools, our way of life. It's a never-ending struggle. They run over us, but we get up and fight 'em again. CCI is our salvation." He pointed out that his home county already has more than twenty hog confinement sites with about eighty buildings, and that more are being planned. "How many are too many?" he asked. Perhaps that is why the Federal

Environmental Protection Agency called Iowa one of the most polluted states in the nation (but that was before they concluded the Clean Air Act did not apply to farms).

Mortensen described the way of life that is being steamrolled, beginning by saying that her children are the fourth generation on her family's farm:

> We want to preserve the peace and calm, the laundry hanging on the line. But now there are close to 40,000 hogs in confinement units within a five-mile radius, and there's a slurry pond a third of a mile up the hill from us. The smell doesn't confine itself to the legally required separation distance, but when we try to fight, we buck up against a lot of powerful opposition. The local newspaper is against us big time. Iowa CCI are our best friends. We would never be able to figure out how to defend ourselves without them.

To which former board member Ferol Wegner added fervently, "we are all human beings," while board member Brenda LaBlanc summed up, "We focus on issues that people are concerned about, building a coalition of urban people, farm people, old people, young people, minority people." And this, of course, is why the Veatch Program supports them.

The link was made personal when Garry Klicker cited a letter from Larry Orr addressed to the Veatch delegation. Orr and his family are members of the Unitarian Universalist Fellowship of Burlington, Iowa, and the letter begins, "Greetings, Fellow UUs." (Actually, most Veatch staff members are not UUs, but they are firmly committed to Unitarian Universalist principles and probably do as much to put them into action as anyone in the denomination.) Orr's letter reads in part,

> Some two years ago, my wife, two children and I moved to an unspoiled, natural corner of Iowa, a wooded area of a county so deep in the backwoods that there is not a single traffic light or franchise of any kind. We moved here to commune with nature, to breathe pure fresh air, to celebrate the seasons, and

to live a simple and natural life. It has been hard but spiritually fulfilling, and we are thriving.

But had it not been for Iowa CCI, all our hopes and joys would have been crushed. About one year ago, we learned from neighbors that a large CAFO [a confined animal feeding operation]—a factory hog farm—was being planned two miles upwind of us. That would have put us into the heavy odor zone, with probable health effects. In addition to the putrid odors, we would have been besieged by the dust of all the trucks carrying hogs, animal food, and manure, which would have gone right by our house.

One of our neighbors had the presence of mind to call Iowa CCI for help, and soon we had a "neighborhood" meeting organized by CCI. It was a wonderful, uplifting experience, and a real exercise in democracy. With Iowa CCI helping us to get organized, and providing good advice based on years of experience in battling for democracy and justice, we were successful in preventing the CAFO from being built. We could not have done it without them!

To make sure that the Veatch visitors—all of them residents of the Greater New York area—knew what a pig looks like, the Iowa hosts arranged a visit to the hog and cattle farm owned by CCI members Frances and Viola Faust. Then, on the next leg of the trip, when the Veatch delegation visited Missouri, the farmers there also arranged a porcine encounter—perhaps anticipating an urban prejudice that if you've seen one pig you've seen them all.

The most significant impression both farms made on the Veatch delegation was what there was *not*: no foul and acrid smell, no sludge pond, no acres of farm land inundated with manure, no pigs in cruel confinement. The three-week-old piglets looked healthy and frisky, even without heavy doses of antibiotics in their feed. The feeder pigs (the adolescents) were fattening up successfully. Although slaughter awaited them once they matured, meanwhile they had a farmer to talk to them and rub their necks—and the CCI to help keep them, and their owners, from being swept away.

## The Urban Dimension

To fulfill its mission, Iowa CCI and its local affiliates have a staff of seventeen, many of whom were in the room that morning of the meeting, together with several CCI members who spoke eloquently of the help the organization had given them. One of them, Ron Branchcomb, says, "this country needs a lot more organizations like CCI. They saved my life." He explained,

> We were victims of predatory lending and were in danger of losing our home when Ameriquest Mortgage threatened to foreclose. It just so happened that we also got a flyer from CCI and something made my wife call them. It was the best phone call we ever made. CCI helped to bring us all together and organize. Up to then people like us had felt ashamed, reluctant to speak out. We formed a task force and CCI put us in touch with the state banking regulators. That brought Ameriquest to the table—something they had refused to do before. After seven months, we got back the money they had stolen from us; a reimbursement check for $26,000. That would never have happened if we hadn't organized with CCI showing us how.

The farmers in the room were the type who wear blue jeans and boots, not as fashion statements but out of necessity. But they do have a style in common with urban youth: They also like to wear baseball caps indoors as well as out. Ferol Wegner, by contrast, was easy to identify as a city dweller. White-haired and gentle, if she represented any stereotype it was that of a grandmother. Her problem was with redlining, the process by which banks and mortgage companies draw a line around a neighborhood where they refuse to make loans because they consider it high risk. Their criteria for this determination are usually that its residents are both poor and members of minorities, often African Americans. Wegner told her story:

> I couldn't buy a house in my own neighborhood, the neighborhood where I grew up. The more I looked into it, the more

I found out that it was a complex situation that involved not only the local banks, so we had to learn step by step, and I don't think we could have done it without CCI. Eventually we were able to form partnerships with some local banks, but we also had to learn to work with Fannie Mae [the federally chartered lending institution]. In fact, I've been going to Washington six times a year ever since.

As a result of these efforts, one of the local banks, First American, has not only been making loans but has actually become an active partner with CCI. It has, for instance, installed motion-activated lights for CCI members at no cost to help keep drug dealers off their property. It has also helped with neighborhood clean-up days when CCI's youth group, Youth Working for Positive Change, helps to pick up trash, and dumpsters are made available to get rid of accumulated junk. Presumably the banking partnership has been mutually beneficial, since another bank, Bankers Trust Company, on its own initiative, has run ads headlined "Citizens for Community Improvement: Thanks for Taking a Stand!" applauding CCI for its efforts to halt predatory lending. "CCI's work will go a long way to ensure that all home buyers will be treated fairly by lenders," the body copy reads, and ends, "We stand with you in the elimination of unfair lending practices."

Shundrea Trotty, youth group coordinator, adds that Bankers Trust, together with the YMCA of Greater Iowa, also supported the youth group's most popular event: the annual "Hidden Heroes Banquet." In 2003, the banquet honored twenty young people. One, now age seventeen, who raised herself in a single-parent home, is now maintaining good grades while working part-time and taking care of her sister's children. Another seventeen-year-old, who grew up in a household where drugs were used routinely, had developed a drug habit by age thirteen. She is now drug-free and an A student and encourages her peers to stay drug-free. A third honoree is only fourteen years old, but in those brief years he has already had several run-ins with the law. He caused so much trouble in school that they used to call his mother every day. He decided to make a change in his life and is now on the honor roll.

## Latinos Unidos

Dawn Jorgensen, a neighborhood leader and member since 1994, went on to describe CCI's history and recent accomplishments. It now has 1,800 members and is still organizing additional chapters; the most recent is Latinos Unidos de CCI in Marshalltown, where the employment situation mirrors that in Omaha but on a smaller scale, with pork rather than beef being packed in a ConAgra (Swift) plant.

Josefina Tejada told of her personal experience:

> I started working at Swift in 1989. The supervisor always treated everybody real bad, but I put up with it until I developed numbness in my hand. They offered me $10,000, but I told them I needed the work and asked for a job I could do. They gave me one that made me work in the cold and lift 70 pounds, so I went to the company doctor and told him I couldn't do it. They said they had no other job for me and I was fired. Because of my injury I can't find other work, but the company claims my injury isn't work-related. Now I'm waiting for a hearing.

Hers is the kind of problem Latinos Unidos was launched to rectify. A bilingual handout explains both the need and the strategy:

> Many times, Latino immigrants feel alone and as if they have no voice in the community. The decisions that most affect them are not made by them but for them, and the rights and needs of the Latino families are lost. In Marshalltown, we want to unite the Latino community. In addition, we want to discover the leadership and power that Latino families have here in Marshalltown. We aim to create a space where Latinos have an opportunity to raise their voices, express their opinions, and be heard. Together we can win!

The handout also explains the process that launched Latinos Unidos. CCI hired an organizer, Anna Galovich, who began in early 2003 by forming a Steering Committee (two members of the clergy and two Latino residents) to help with fundraising, do research, and give advice. The critical first step was to connect with the Latino community by holding some sixty to eighty one-on-one meetings to hear problems and concerns firsthand. That, in turn, helped identify the fifteen to twenty potential leaders who then made up the organizing committee. They proposed five issues to work on immediately. Three issues surrounded the Swift plant—wrongful termination, unsafe working conditions, and abusive treatment—and two issues concerned the community—learning English, and violence and drug use in the schools.

A kickoff meeting then elected leaders and began to address these issues. The committee statement concludes with a pledge: "We will listen to you! We will not tell you how to run your group. You make the decisions and you make the changes." This statement expresses perfectly the basic principle of community organization and democratic action that the Veatch Program works so hard to encourage. Most important, it is a strategy that often leads to success. In the Chesterfield neighborhood, for instance, under the slogan, "Don't let the city dump on us," CCI conducted a campaign against a human sludge storage facility located within three hundred feet of people's homes. Dawn Jorgensen reported that the foul odors made these homes unlivable. Starting with one city councilman, the neighbors succeeded in getting the council to conduct a study, proved that the facility had been illegally built, made the city empty it, and finally got the council to approve a relocation program for the affected residents. It took about a year of research, presentations, and protest demonstrations. As Jorgensen stressed, the neighbors won their own victory—but they could not have done it if CCI had not shown them how.

# Kansas City Congregational Partners
## *Bridging the Racial and Religious Divide*

AFTER NEBRASKA AND Iowa, the Veatch delegation made several stops in Missouri, starting with a lavish breakfast at Simpson House of Kansas City All Souls Unitarian Universalist Church. An architectural landmark next door to the church, this elegant 1909 stone mansion had been acquired and restored by the All Souls congregation to meet not only its own needs but also to provide office space for nonprofit organizations.

Gathered in Simpson House when the Veatch visitors arrived were some forty participants in the Kansas City Congregational Partners Program (CPP), which seeks to help congregations of different faiths and ethnicities build personal and community service relationships. Over the years, the Unitarian Universalist Funding Program, which in turn receives Veatch support, has funneled some $20,000 to CPP, with the All Souls church serving as applicant, conduit, and additional supporter. This triangular relationship explains why the Veatch delegation came to visit and why so many All Souls members were in attendance, leading the group in singing "Morning Has Broken" from the UU hymnal.

The participants represented other partnership congregations and the staff of Harmony, an umbrella Kansas City organization dedicated to promoting appreciation of cultural diversity that provides administrative and programmatic support for CPP.

This time no boots were in evidence, and the only jeans were tailored and neatly pressed, for this group was predominantly made up of urban and suburban church women (and a few men) reporting on the highly personal relationships they had built across racial and religious barriers—the kind of barriers that exist in all cities and are only rarely pierced or even acknowledged.

Leading off the discussion were Diane Hershberger, Harmony executive director, and Janet Brown Moss, program coordinator. They explained how the partnership program had been launched in 1997 in response to a recommendation by the Mayor's Task Force on Race Relations, "for the purpose of improving the lives of our city's children and bringing racial harmony." The proposal encouraged "not only dialogue, but also bringing together resources for common community services." Rev. John Weston, then the All Souls minister, and Imam Bilal Muhammed of the Al Inshirah Islamic Center led the way in forming CPP. Its mission then as now was "to assist congregations of different denominations, faiths, and ethnicity to build relationships of trust, and unite to serve our metropolitan community."

There are currently sixteen active partnerships, at least five of them involved in community service. The goal for 2003 was to form a minimum of four new partnerships, and to involve five more of the existing ones in community service programs.

Speaking as an African American and Muslim, Imam Bilal Muhammed spoke eloquently about the program's twin objectives of breaking down both racial and religious barriers. The partnership program, he said, had helped to build bridges between members of the Islamic Center, St. Monica Catholic Church, and Congregation Beth Torah; it had also reconnected at least some of those who had left Kansas City for the suburbs as part of "white flight" with those of other colors they had left behind. Its effectiveness in bringing people together was especially vital after September 11, 2001, when American Muslims were often the targets of suspicion and hostility.

## Uprooting a Racist Past

Going around the room, other speakers (both black and white, representing most of the thirty-plus congregations in the partnership) echoed Imam Bilal Mohammed's positive evaluation. As Kathy Butterfield of All Souls, one of the two Unitarian Universalist churches in the program, explained,

> The program has provided an opportunity for our congregation, which is largely white, to become acquainted with people of different racial and religious backgrounds in peer relationships. Our partner church is Ward Chapel African Methodist Episcopal church. We have had pulpit and choir exchanges, and come together for joint retreats. They invited us to a fish fry and we held a brunch. It has built a peer relationship that would not likely have come about any other way.

Janet Brown Moss elaborated:

> Partnership programs have also given us opportunities to learn from local historians about the history of African Americans in Kansas City, and about other faiths from the clergy of Al Inshirah Islamic Center, Congregation Beth Torah, St. Monica Catholic Church, New Hope Missionary Baptist, and Saint Ann's/Saint Cyril's Catholic Church, as well as St. Andrew United Methodist and North Oak Christian Churches.

> I am touched and energized as I watch increasing numbers of individuals venture into places they would likely not go were it not for this program. I've had the chance to attend a Muslim wedding, to watch the gleaming faces of white women from the suburbs joining their [black] sisters at Missionary Baptist Church to sing in a large choir for the Women's Day service,

and to take photos while members of a white and a black congregation do face painting and craft-making during parties they host for children at an emergency shelter.

One such encounter took place recently at a gathering of the St. Anne's/St. Cyril's and New Hope Missionary Baptist partnership, when Alversia Brown Pettigrew read her poem, "Memories of a Neck Child." She had lived in a part of Independence known as "The Neck," a close-knit, primarily African American community that was torn apart by urban renewal projects in the 1960s. Other typical Harmony projects include a cleanup day at a city park, a workplace diversity leadership forum, and a "hate-busters" van trip to the cultural extremes of Kansas City, widely considered one of the most segregated in the nation.

The roots of Missouri racism go back to well before the Civil War, when parts of the state were culturally more like the Old South than the Midwest. Indeed, in the 1850s, the small town of Weston, on the outskirts of Kansas City, was a base for the "Border Ruffians," the notorious proslavery thugs who fought to turn Kansas into a slave state. To that end, David Rice Atchison, one of their leaders, said, "We will be compelled to shoot, burn, and hang." And that's precisely what they did.

The Congregational Partners Program is an important part of the attempt to heal the wounds that still remain. As the first partnership, the All Souls/Ward Chapel alliance has served as a model, consistently creating opportunities for its members to participate in joint activities. This is how Butterfield, cochair of the All Souls/Ward Chapel partnership planning group, sums up what has been achieved in the way of community service and the fight for racial justice:

> Together with Ward Chapel, we give parties and provide activities for the children of the Salvation Army children's shelter. Recently, we took some twenty children from the shelter to the zoo, together with kids from both our congregations. There is no other way in which our children would

have this opportunity. Together with Ward Chapel members, our members several days every week assist in the operation of a soup kitchen, feeding homeless and poor people and delivering meals to shut-ins.

Through the partnership program we can also provide community leadership. There was a situation when hate mail was sent to several black ministers. All Souls called upon Congregational Partners to help draw in people from numerous congregations from all over the city to lead a campaign to make a public statement repudiating the hate mail. We collected money and signatures for a full-page ad in the *Kansas City Star* saying we wouldn't stand for that kind of action, and close to two thousand people signed up.

One of the implicit ground rules of the partnership is that there can be no attempt at proselytizing; but neither is there any attempt to hide theological differences among the congregations. All Souls and its AME partners, for instance, have held retreats at which each congregation explained its denominational origins and core beliefs. "There may have been a little bit of bemusement in both congregations," Kathy Butterfield reflects, "but the exchanges were very well received. I don't think anyone felt put upon, though I suspect that there may be a few people in each group who privately take a dim view of aspects of the other's theological position. Generally, everyone feels that 'this is your way and this is our way,' so we sample each other's approaches without anyone trying to shove anything down anyone else's throat."

The unabashedly UU invocation by the host minister, Rev. Jim Eller, serves as a good example of this nonassertive but unapologetic way of self-identification and mutual respect. It works because people of many denominations feel a need to break out of their denominational boundaries, to acknowledge that a common humanity trumps parochial loyalties. Or as a Congregational Partners Program statement puts it, a need that "can be felt in our yearning to build relationships of trust and care with people of faiths and cultures from whom we have become separated. Let's learn, celebrate and work together in each of our neighborhoods, creating community healing for adults and youth."

The statement concludes with a quotation from an Australian aborigine woman: "If you have come to help me, you are wasting my time. But if you have come because your liberation is bound up with mine, then let us work together."

# Grass Roots Organizing
## *Building Ladders Out of Poverty*

THE INTERDEPENDENCE of rural and urban justice was made highly visible when the Veatch delegates arrived at the Columbia headquarters of the Missouri Rural Crisis Center (MRCC).

The faces of those waiting to meet them came in all colors, but their T-shirts were all bright yellow. They were being worn by both the representatives of Grass Roots Organizing (GRO), a social justice organization led by women on public assistance in mid-Missouri, and their MRCC hosts. MRCC, while focused primarily on the problems of family farmers, has made great efforts to build alliances with other progressive organizations such as GRO.

Headquartered in nearby Mexico, the GRO delegates had come to the MRCC office for the convenience of the Veatch visitors. More to the point, the choice of meeting place reflected the close working relationship of the two organizations, one mostly black, the other predominantly white; one mostly urban, the other primarily rural. Once again the organizational story was told in personal terms through the voices of staff and volunteers. Robin Acree, the executive director of GRO, spoke with great passion about her own experience.

> I was trapped in an abusive marriage, and even though I was the victim, it landed me in jail. I lost my job and wound up a

single mother with three kids, living in public housing. It was a great struggle, but eventually I managed to go to college, and that in turn helped me get a job with the city of Mexico. Having fought my own way out of poverty, I wasn't going to turn my back on those I'd left behind, and I was one of six people who started GRO. Our mission from the beginning was to create a grassroots mechanism that gives voice to individuals and communities in the pursuit of economic justice and human rights. We now have close to 300 members. I'd sum up what we do as creating ladders to help people climb out of poverty.

Equally eloquent voices followed:

- "I used to be a Republican, but a motorcycle accident showed me that sometimes circumstances make you dependent on the help of others. One person doesn't get heard, but when we all speak with one voice, they have to listen to us."
- "People power is the answer, because we operate on a shoestring." (GRO has only one full-time staff member, the executive director, and three part-time organizers. Volunteers are its lifeblood.) "We change people's lives."
- "As a kid I used to believe in the pledge of allegiance. I still believe in justice, but I no longer believe that there is justice for all. It's something we have to fight for."
- "Going to the National People's Action with GRO changed my life. It was tremendously empowering."
- "In our trailer park there were problems with drugs and untreated sewage, and a complete lack of services. Somebody called the fire department, but the fire truck never made it to the trailer because it fell in a hole. But when people get together and fight, we can win—even if it takes a year or more. Now things aren't ideal, but thanks to GRO they're a lot better than they were."

Robin Acree sums up: "We challenge so much that otherwise would not be challenged at all," and she cites one of GRO's most dramatic efforts. Thirty-seven volunteers went by chartered bus to attend an "economic summit" in Texas. For three days, together with members of other grassroots groups, they went from Dallas to Waco to Crawford to deliver a single message: What about the *rest* of us? That got no immediate response from the power elite, but it did generate national media attention, as did the presentation of simulated checks made out to George W. Bush and Dick Cheney, which made the pages of *USA Today*.

Coverage of such demonstrations can succeed only with media savvy. The importance of training to use the media to best advantage was one of the reasons why the Unitarian Universalist Fund for a Just Society (again dispensing money provided by the Veatch Program) provided GRO with a $5,000 challenge grant. It represented only a little over 5 percent of its $181,000 budget, but helped supplement membership dues of $1 to $5 a month, depending on ability to pay. Such challenge grants reflect a basic Veatch principle that membership support, even if limited by poverty, must be one of the demonstrations of commitment and active participation. The premise is that sooner or later outside support will stop, and at that point a successful organization has to be able to function on its own.

Grass Roots Organizing volunteers participate in five action teams:

- *Rescue Our Teeth (ROT)* fights for low-income access to dental and other health care.

- *Family Income Support Team (FIST)* tackles the problems families encounter because of the expiration of Temporary Assistance for Needy Families, which is supposed to ease the transition from welfare and child support, but cannot work when there are no jobs available.

- *Food Stamps* seeks to improve access to food benefits for hungry families by fighting a punitive state regulation that says children under six do not qualify for this vital support.

• *Tenants Rights* helps tenants faced with evictions or other unfair treatment.

• *Utility* combats the burden of high utility bills and recent increases in late fees.

Nor are these the only ways that increasingly restrictive regulations and budget cuts hurt Missouri's most vulnerable residents. Take Medicaid. According to GRO, some 96,000 Missouri adults and 84,000 children are in danger of losing their benefits unless current policies are revised. GRO has been trying to communicate to policy makers and the public at large the message that "These Cuts Won't Heal!" and as GRO leader Amy Pauley says, "Do they want us to just die and go away? Without access to medications and treatment I cannot survive."

Grass Root Organizing and its allies did succeed in at least partially reversing a drastic reduction in the monthly checks for residents on General Relief, but the pattern in Missouri, as in most states, has been for legislators to refuse to raise taxes (or in some states even to cut them), and instead to bridge budget shortfalls at the expense of people at the bottom of the economic heap. It is a great help, therefore, when other citizens with grievances—such as the farmer members of MRCC—join them in their protests.

## Finding Allies

As further demonstration of the broad perspective of the Missouri Rural Crisis Center, its presentation was divided between two settings: one rural, at its Columbia headquarters, the other urban, at a Kansas City African American church. In fact, MRCC's commitment also has an international dimension, as became very visible when Rhonda Perry, MRCC program director, welcomed the Veatch visitors.

Explaining why she was wearing an elegant, citified dress while the other farmers looked like farmers, she said that she was just back from an Oxfam meeting in Nicaragua and had not yet had time to go home to change. The purpose of the Oxfam meeting was to devise strategies for shielding Latin American peasants from the impact of U.S. farm policies that, by exporting subsidized farm products, are also exporting the assault on rural families.

But that's getting ahead of the MRCC story.

Roger Allison, MRCC's executive director, explained why the meeting was being held at a preponderantly black inner city church. "Farmers can't win justice in isolation from other segments of society," he says. Roger—no one ever seemed to use his last name—is more than just charismatic; he is larger than life. Bearded, barrel-chested, well over six feet tall, he has a voice to match his proportions, and his associates, even his wife Rhonda Perry, kidded him gently about turning his five agenda minutes into as long as it took for someone to stop him. But what he had to say was well worth the extra time:

> When we organized MRCC in 1985, it was because the farm crisis of the '80s was driving family farmers into bankruptcy. Hundreds of thousands of farmers were in danger of losing their land. We didn't get very far until we discovered that we had a common interest with other social justice causes, and Jesse Jackson was one of the few public figures who was willing to come out to support us. As we explained to him, this group of white farmers was a social justice organization, not just an economic pressure group. Another supporter was Willie Nelson, whose Farm Aid raised the money to get us started.

> In Western Kansas and Idaho in those days, farmers were so desperate that they were easy prey for what were really fascist organizations. With no one else apparently ready to care about them, they were beginning to listen to the American Nazi Party and the Posse Comitatus. It was a scary time.

Roger Allison became an activist when he got arrested trying to stop the foreclosure of his parents' farm. He helped them go to court and eventually win their case. But he didn't stop there; he realized that the threat wasn't purely economic but came from social policies that considered family farmers "excess resources" who had to give way for "more efficient" methods of producing food. And so he began to fight and he has been fighting ever since.

Bryce Oates of the MRCC staff picked up the story. He related how MRCC became a membership organization in 1987; grew to its current strength of fifty-five hundred member families; established twelve chapters, and thereby became the leading progressive farm organization in Missouri.

"Missouri is a major agricultural state," he explained, "second only to Texas in most crops." But, like Roger Allison, he stressed that farmers could not win their battles without allies. "In the early to mid-eighties, farm people were going hungry, but many of them were too proud and individualistic to ask for help or to organize."

The Missouri Rural Crisis Center offered them an alternative to quietly leaving the land and sinking into poverty. It showed them that they could save their way of life by organizing, a useful lesson when the next crisis struck: the invasion of industrial farms in the late 1980s and early 1990s. Then came the North Atlantic Free Trade Agreement (NAFTA), another disaster not only for farmers in this country but especially in Latin America. First, the industrial farms drove down commodity prices. Then NAFTA left Mexico defenseless against imports that undersold their locally raised produce. The MRCC leaders understood that to survive they had to build bridges to other social justice organizations both at home and abroad. They found allies in labor unions, civil rights, and gay and lesbian organizations—wherever any group was battling for justice, equity, and fairness. As its mission statement says, "The mission of the Missouri Rural Crisis Center is to preserve family farms, promote stewardship of the land and environmental integrity, and strive for economic and social justice by building unity and mutual understanding among diverse groups, both rural and urban."

## Standing Up to Corporate Interests

MRCC is currently fighting against cuts in Medicaid, food stamps, and health care, and just about every other social benefit program you can name. But the most immediate threat to hog farmers is the Pork Checkoff.

Although a U.S. district judge has ruled this system "unconstitutional and rotten," the National Pork Producers Council, with the help of the Bush Administration's Department of Agriculture, is fighting to preserve it. Briefly, it works as follows: Every time a hog is sold, the seller is assessed 40 cents per $100 of sale value. Over the years, the bulk of the money has gone to the National Pork Producers Council and its state associations, which are dominated by corporate farm interests. NPPC has used the millions generated by the check-off to run its "The Other White Meat" campaign—but only factory-produced pork is white; pasture-raised pork is on the pink or reddish side. This has been another major factor in driving family farmers out of business: Between 1985 when the campaign started and 2002, the number of hog farms went from some 390,000 to fewer than 82,000, even though the number of pigs raised stayed about the same.

In 1998, the Campaign for Family Farms—a coalition including both MRCC and Iowa Citizens for Community Improvement (ICCI), as well as the Minnesota Land Stewardship Project—launched a successful petition drive demanding a national referendum about the check-off. The Pork Council spent $4 million to defeat them; nonetheless hog farmers voted by 53 percent to 47 percent to stop the check-off. With President Clinton still in the White House, then Secretary Dan Glickman ordered its termination, but when he was succeeded by Secretary Veneman after the 2000 election, she reversed his order. "It's nothing short of tyrannical to continue to force hog farmers to pay millions of dollars into a program that ultimately leads to their demise," says Iowa farmer Larry Ginter of ICCI. Together with Rhonda Perry and two Minnesota farmers he took the USDA to court. They won in district court but the Bush Administration appealed, and so the check-off continues, pending further rulings. As Rhonda Perry says,

> We're going to see this through. Hog farmers should not be forced to pay into a mandatory check-off that supports Smithfield, Cargill, and Hormel, and hurts independent

family farmers. We believe justice will be served and this unfair and failed pork check-off will be ended because it is unconstitutional.

Nor is the check-off setback the only way family farmers have been hurt by the change in Washington's balance of power. In 1996, Congress included an Environmental Quality Incentives Program (EQIP) in that year's farm bill to protect both family farmers and the environment. In 2002, Congress revised the bill to conform with the wishes of the industrial farm lobby. The late Senator Paul Wellstone of Minnesota fought hard against these changes, but the majority did the lobby's bidding.

A current legislative battle, still to be decided, is a bill introduced by Senator Grassley (Republican of Iowa) to ban packer ownership of livestock—an essential measure if the spread of factory farms is to be at least slowed down. A few statistics gathered by MRCC show why such a ban is needed:

- In 2002, the top six meat-packer/pork producing corporations owned more than one-fifth of the U.S. sow herd.
- Between 1993 and 2002, 65 percent of hog producers went out of business.
- In the same nine years, the producers' share of the retail dollar plummeted from 37 cents to 23 cents. But the consumer did not benefit: at the same time, the retail price of pork went up 35 percent.

All these struggles are part of MRCC's long-range goal to establish a food security policy that will preserve family farming as a key component of American agriculture, and enable farmers in other countries to remain on their land and not have to seek menial and exploitative jobs in the United States. because they can't compete with subsidized U.S. imports. To achieve that goal, it is necessary not only to let family farmers keep farming but to find ways for them to market their products. That discussion was the focus of the following day's tour of the Patchwork Family Farms packing plant, a grassroots cooperative organized by MRCC.

## Patchwork Family Farms

In notable contrast to those of its mass production competitors, there is nothing offensive about the Patchwork packing plant. Spotlessly clean and virtually odorless, it is a self-contained facility capable of every operation that turns hogs into packaged meat products except the initial slaughtering. These products are then shipped out on trucks that proudly proclaim "Patchwork Family Farms—Working Together to Make a Difference."

Patchwork provides family farmers with a market outlet, featuring quality products at fair prices. To understand why this is necessary, one needs to take a look at the manifold ways in which factory farming threatens the survival of the family farmer. It leads to overproduction, which drives down market prices. Because of the way factory hog operations wreck the air and water quality of surrounding areas, they often make neighboring family farms unlivable and drive down property values. But perhaps the most devastating blow is the way their corporate competitors interfere with the family farmers' ability to market their products. Because most factory farms are owned by or contracted to multinational corporations, which in turn deal with multinational supermarket chains, they are able to lock family farmers out of their traditional market outlets. The neighborhood butcher is a thing of the past.

Patchworks provides an alternative by putting co-op members in control of their own processing and marketing. Oxfam, an early funder, uses the example of Carl Weihardt to explain how it works:

> Carl has been raising hogs all his life on his piece of land in central Missouri—a state known for its quality pigs. Hog raising has always been the mainstay of Missouri's family farmers . . . [and] Missouri farmers were proud of their hogs, up until the last few years. Recently, the hog market has been going haywire. "It's like riding a roller coaster, got down to 8 cents a pound," lamented Carl. "Got so a bottle of medicine cost more than what a fat hog will bring you. . . . It just makes me mad that the big guys come in here and make it hard on us small guys to try to keep the farm viable"

Carl also says, "I just kinda got a love for hogs," contrasting his concern for the animals with the way they are treated on factory farms. Factory hogs are kept indoors and need daily doses of antibiotics to keep them from succumbing to the unsanitary conditions. "A hog is made to be outside in the dirt," Carl adds. "When they're inside and never see daylight, that'd be just like putting me in jail."

Then he explains why the consumer also has a stake in what happens to the hogs, saying, "I am concerned about what the American people eat. I wouldn't want them to eat anything that I wouldn't put on the table for my family." Anyone who is concerned can follow the advice of Roger Allison. The way to detect factory-raised pork in your own kitchen, he says, is to put it in a pan with a little water and turn the heat on low. "After about five minutes, lift the lid and smell. You'll know."

Another advantage, as the Veatch team found out at a lunch hosted by MRCC at the Columbia Unitarian Universalist Church, is that Patchwork pork tastes better. But the basic issue is the one expressed by Mary Jo Lyon, a Patchwork producer: "Because we raise hogs for Patchworks Family Farms we can stay on our farm."

After lunch, the presentations continued, including an explanation of the way Patchwork distributes its products to over fifty mid-Missouri grocery stores and restaurants. It also maintains a retail outlet in Columbia, organizes consumer co-ops, and provides food to various community groups and churches in Kansas City and St. Louis.

Jim Compton, a board member and founder, sums up the Patchwork history:

> We started Patchwork Family Farmers just about ten years ago, and our food co-op now has eleven chapters to which we make regular deliveries. Actually, we got the idea from an emergency food distribution program we ran after the 1993 flood that gradually evolved into a co-op. The program works because we pay our producers more than they could get anywhere else by setting a minimum payment at market

price plus 15 percent. Our gross sales this year [2003] is running at $350,000, and we're aiming at $375,000 next year. That
means we need more outlets for our products—we actually
have farmers waiting to join but right now we can't handle
any more. So we need to sign up more restaurants and grocery stores, and expand our mail order business.

The food co-ops are run by volunteers, who then sign up
friends and neighbors with whom they share their shipments. But
volunteers do far more. In one county they arrange for surprise
helicopter overflights to keep an eye on factory farms. At the state
capital they demonstrate on behalf of such legislative priorities as
requiring a quarter-mile buffer between farm structures and
property lines—federal regulations permit them to be built right
on the property line.

Another participant at the meeting is Margot McMillen, whose
determination to fight back was aroused when a factory farm
opened right next door to her. "Our first demonstration was very
polite," she recalls, "so nobody paid attention. The next time, we
unfurled some 500 yards of petitions from the balcony [of the legis-
lature]. That woke up the media. Even so, it took some five months
of intensive grassroots organizing before we won that fight."

## The Campaign for Family Farms and the Environment

While MRCC tackles many such immediate needs, it also concentrates on changing the systemic causes of Missouri's problems,
and that calls for alliances with other citizens' organizations to gain
the clout that only strength in numbers can deliver. For instance, it is
one of the five statewide organizations (Iowa Citizens for Community
Improvement is another) that make up the Campaign for Family
Farms and the Environment (CFFE). Organized in 1995, CFFE is
putting its collective power behind the campaigns to end the pork
check-off and to ban packer ownership of livestock.

Furthermore, CFFE serves as a clearinghouse so that members
can learn from each other. Ten MRCC members and Patchwork

Family Farm producers recently traveled to Minnesota to share their experience in marketing family farm products and, in return, toured the Minnesota Sustainable Swine Research Center to learn about new techniques in sustainable hog production.

Meanwhile, MRCC is pursuing the goals it holds in common with its urban and overseas allies. Bill Christison, the organization's president, underlines the importance of such bridge-building:

> We also belong to the National Family Farm Coalition, which has fifteen state affiliates, giving us an important presence in Washington. One of our current battles is to keep country of origin labeling from being derailed. In early 2003, Congress adopted a new law that fresh meat, fish, and produce be labeled by country of origin starting in September 2004. That would give us a tool for educating consumers about the importance of keeping US farmers on the land, and to keep big importers from manipulating the marketplace with cheap foreign imports. Unfortunately, the giant meat packers and commodity groups, with the help of the Department of Agriculture, are trying to stop the program in its tracks.
>
> We're also active on the international front, since all of the world's agriculture is interconnected. I've just come back from a meeting in Copenhagen of Via Campesima, which has millions of members around the world who are fighting for food autonomy. One of the big battles is to fight against genetic engineering of crops. Education is a big part of that issue. For instance, we have proof that raising Roundup Ready soybeans actually costs more, and not only are costs up but yields are down. So we're putting together a farmer-to-farmer coalition to promote policies that benefit the farmers and not the big multinational chemical companies.

All these activities explain why the Veatch Program has supported Missouri Rural Crisis Center since 1990, starting with a modest $15,000 grant the first year and climbing to a cumulative thirteen-year total of $345,000 by 2003. This is also why Willie

Nelson, president of Farm Aid, says, "Farm Aid supports MRCC in their struggle. This is a classic example of why Farm Aid came into existence—to keep big corporate farms from running over the little people."

The MRCC visit ended with another stop at a family farm. All these pigs, too, seemed happy, snuffling around in the mud, and the chickens had their beaks intact. (Factory-bred chickens need to be de-beaked to keep them from bloodying each other in their confinement). As for the farmer, he was deeply appreciative about the way MRCC and Patchwork Family Farms are making it possible for him to stay on as the third generation owner of his property.

Then it was on to St. Louis—with only a slight delay to talk a state trooper out of a speeding ticket. He seemed puzzled by the multicultural makeup of the van's occupants, peering repeatedly at the Japanese, Puerto Rican, and white male and female faces, but he settled for a warning. Outwardly, at least, the Veatch folks didn't seem to him to look like troublemakers. Little did he guess that they were in fact in pursuit of a deeply subversive agenda—to change a system rigged against the poor and powerless.

# Jobs with Justice
## *Promoting Fairness in the Workplace*

IN 2002, JOBS WITH JUSTICE (JwJ), a national organization with some forty chapters, received a $65,000 grant from the Veatch Program to help ensure that working people receive a living wage and are treated with fairness and respect. To this end, JwJ enlists labor unions and civil rights and community organizations, as well as faith-based and student groups. It needs and welcomes all the allies it can get.

For its final Midwest stop, the Veatch delegation visited St. Louis Jobs with Justice. St. Louis presents a special challenge. On the one hand, it has one of the highest densities of union membership in the country, with almost one household in five covered by collective bargaining agreements. On the other, the city's population is about 51 percent African American, and many blacks perceive the union leadership to be part of the white power structure that has been ignoring their needs or even holding them down. Because southern Missouri has a strong segregationist/Bible Belt tradition, little can be achieved until the working population becomes less polarized, and St. Louis JwJ is dedicated to healing this split.

It was significant, therefore, that the meeting with JwJ took place in the office of the Organization for Black Struggle (OBS), and that Kalimu Endesha, an OBS leader, was the first speaker. An impressive six-footer with dreadlocks to his shoulders, Endesha spoke about a significant victory achieved by his twenty-three-year old organization when it recently helped defeat an incumbent city councilman who, though black, had done little for the community. OBS achieved this hard-fought victory, Endesha explained, despite the opposition of the mayor, white labor, and the *St. Louis Post-Dispatch*, the city's leading newspaper. "Thousands of dollars were poured into the ward, hoping to drown the grassroots efforts of the Boyd [anti-incumbent] forces," Endesha said, "but the ward rose to a new day and finally began to feel empowered again."

He then ticked off the issues still on the OBS agenda, starting with the formation of a civilian oversight board to stop police brutality, a campaign actively supported by Jobs with Justice. As Janey Archey, a white JwJ supporter, points out, thirty-seven people were killed by the police in recent years—and every one of them was black. "Let's come together to win fair wages and benefits for all workers," she adds.

That, of course, is what Jobs with Justice is all about.

In the words of Joan Suarez, an international officer of UNITE (the clothing workers union) and coordinator of JwJ's Workers Rights Board, "How do you pay the bills when you make $5.45 an hour?" Writing in the *Post-Dispatch*, she cites the data from the Economic Policy Institute that a family of five needs an annual income of $40,861 to meet basic needs, adding,

> The United Sates is a proud nation where the overwhelming majority believes that any person who works hard should live in dignity. This is not the case for too many people in this city and in this nation. These few steps [that JwJ has proposed] could alter the balance back in favor of the hard-working people.

The Workers Rights Board is near the top of the JwJ agenda. Its intent is to "create a place where prominent community leaders can use their moral authority to assist workers in distress," according to

Lara Granich, JwJ's director and only full-time organizer. At a recent public hearing the board recruited some fifty community leaders, including elected officials, clergy, and academics, who listened to the personal stories of low-paid workers. One of them, Vinnie Sharp, said, "I work in a low-wage industry right here in St. Louis. We make shoelaces. I make $5.45 an hour. We don't have much in health benefits. We don't have a pension either, and I can't even think about retirement."

Another said, "For fourteen years I have worked to keep buildings clean. For my efforts, I am paid only $6.40 an hour, with benefits offered to me but too expensive for me to accept. I am seventy-two years old and lucky enough not to have to feed more than myself on this pitiful wage, because I could not do it."

St. Louis Jobs with Justice helped mobilize support for the Justice for Janitors campaign for the sake of underpaid workers like these. Local union leaders reported to the Veatch delegation how the initial success of JwJ was beginning to bridge the gap between traditional organized labor and underpaid workers. Charles Hatcher, the white organizing director of the Service Employees Local 50, described how the union, on behalf of some three thousand janitors, demanded that cleaning companies raise salaries by $1 per hour per year, set up a paid healthcare plan, and beef up the pension plan. The Contract Cleaners Association, representing eight of the major cleaning companies, didn't take the demands seriously at first. To generate public awareness, JwJ awarded the association its 2002 "Grinch of the Year Award" as the worst employer in the St. Louis area. That got publicity but did not generate much pressure. The pressure began to build only when janitors and their union and JwJ supporters took to the streets. They held lunchtime rallies in downtown St. Louis. The newspapers described participants as "250 chanting, singing people" who held signs reading "No More Poverty Wages" and wore purple T-shirts that proudly proclaimed "Jobs with Justice."

Significantly, not all of the rally speakers were janitors or union leaders. JwJ member Lori Reed, for instance, is a community supporter from the American Friends Service Committee who said: "People who work for a living deserve not to have to struggle." Eventually, this kind of community support succeeded in obtaining better contracts with most of the major cleaning companies. At St. Louis University, for example, the old contract called for an hourly minimum wage of $5.25. Under the new contract it is $7.25. As Mary Fox told the Veatch visitors, "At first our members were scared. They knew they needed better pay and health benefits, but they felt threatened. It wasn't until Jobs with Justice showed them they had community support that they dared to speak out."

## Building Long-Term Coalitions

Meanwhile, new problems keep cropping up. According to Roosevelt Stewart, president of the American Postal Workers local, his members tend to feel that if they pay their dues the union will take care of them, and so they have been relatively passive. For them, therefore, the current attempts by both the Bush and state administrations to privatize the government workforce and contract with nonunion companies serves as a wake-up call, but because of their past inertia they don't believe they can have an impact. They need to witness a few more worker victories to change that attitude, Stewart feels, which is why this relatively powerful union decided to help the janitors. It was not only a demonstration of labor solidarity, but a matter of immediate self-interest.

A recent victory for fairness was the four-to-one vote in favor of a living wage ordinance in a city referendum. The vote was the culmination of a Living Wage Campaign spearheaded by the local chapter of Association of Community Organizations for Reform Now (ACORN) which brought together a coalition of unions and religious and community organizations. JwJ's most visible contribution was a Tour of Shame—one of its "street heat" tactics—shining the spotlight of publicity on area employers paying poverty-level wages while receiving tax support. JwJ also helped organize the coalition that prevented the closing down of

ConnectCare, a network of health clinics in medically underserved communities.

One of the biggest challenges is to make sure that these coalitions are more than ad hoc alliances that concentrate on a single issue and then disperse. As Charlie Hatcher points out,

> The importance of Jobs with Justice is that it is an ongoing coalition, so that when an issue comes up, we can, for instance, turn out hundreds of supporters for the janitors.

> The challenge for a union like ours is this: How do we get more members involved so we can prove to them that we can make a change? But how can we make a change until we get more members involved? Well, we now have janitors as part of the union's leadership and that's thanks to the success we scored with the help of Jobs with Justice. We're for real now, as the big boys are beginning to find out.

> Another plus offered by Jobs with Justice is that it's a clearing house of information, so everyone can know what's going on. By avoiding duplication of effort, it brings greater efficiency to the use of limited resources. But above all, it creates connections, and that is making the growth of Jobs with Justice exponential. Not only is it helping to overcome the split between labor unions and the black community, but it is building all kinds of cross-cultural connections that are making all of us much stronger collectively.

Steve Hollis is a one-person symbol of such cross-cultural connections. He is president of the American Federation of Government Employees Local 3354 (which represents USDA employees), recording secretary of Jobs with Justice, and a board member of the Missouri Rural Crisis Center. In this triple capacity he took the lead in building ties between his union and the National Family Farm Coalition. "We need to build a progressive political coalition in the state and in St. Louis," he says, seconding Hatcher's statement: "We all have our own priority issues, and it used to be that when our issue got settled, we'd go home until the next issue came up. What's driving this organization is the commitment by all of us to stick around and help each other—to build this organization and make it a major force in the community."

Rhonda Perry of Missouri Rural Crisis Center gives this strategy a ringing endorsement:

> We have decided to join and actively support the work of St. Louis Area Jobs with Justice to build a strong solidarity coalition among labor, community-based, faith-based, and student activists in the metro St. Louis area.
>
> We have made this decision because St. Louis JwJ is demonstrating its ability to effectively educate and organize St. Louis area labor unions, organizations from diverse components of the St. Louis community, including immigrant and African American organizations, and is reaching out to bring in the faith-based community as well. They help us by providing successful organizing and media support for the Fair Trade campaign . . . and they have also provided assistance to MRCC in media work in the St. Louis area.
>
> This growing St. Louis solidarity coalition for economic and social justice has reached out to MRCC so that together we can build mutual understanding and respect between urban and rural activists in Missouri.

Fostering mutual support is a basic Veatch Program strategy, which is one reason why both St. Louis Jobs with Justice and MRCC have received Veatch grants. The St. Louis Metropolitan Congregations United is another ally, working to get past the religious community's current pattern of each denomination working separately—or sitting on the sidelines. Hatcher says bluntly, "They need to get together."

Lara Granich emphasizes how St. Louis Jobs with Justice is promoting cooperative and coordinated action. "Our long-term goal," she says, "is to build a network of allies. To do so, we need first to win some victories around single issues. The second step is to organize St. Louis workers. What you have heard today are vivid illustrations of how we have advanced on both fronts. The help we have received from the Veatch Program has been invaluable in achieving the progress we have made, and we want you to know how much we appreciate it."

This brings to full circle a point Margie Fine raised during the Veatch delegation's visit: "Members of the UU Shelter Rock congregation sometimes ask: 'What happens to the Veatch money?' We go on these site visits to get the answers. That's why we are here today."

## Getting Started in an Anti-union State

Texas offers another example of the union/Jobs with Justice alliance. Danny Fetonte, Southwest area director of the Communications Workers of America (CWA), has taken on the additional task of helping JwJ get firmly established in his five-state region.

St. Louis at least has a strong union base, while Texas is anti-union country. That is why, even more than in St. Louis, the key to success for Fetonte is the forming of coalitions. Indeed, JwJ describes itself as a "coalition of labor unions and religious, civil rights, women's, student, farm, and community organizations working together on the local level to defend and expand the rights of working people." In 2002, the Veatch Program allocated a $65,000 grant to the Washington office to help this effort; it also supports the Austin-based Texas effort.

"We Are the Majority," proclaims a JwJ publication, which also states,

> Our economy is being destroyed by a new generation of corporate robber barons and the elected officials who do their bidding. To them, greed is more important than need. Working people become disposable items. Our standard of living is slashed, our health benefits cut, and job security eliminated. Alone against these forces it is tough—and usually impossible —to win. Together we are the majority. Together we can start to win again.

The formula, according to JwJ, is straightforward but not simple. First, unions must mobilize their own members. Second, they
must make it clear that job security, health care, and a decent stan-
dard of living for all Americans are community issues, vital not
just for the individual workers but for the nation at large. As a
corollary, Jobs with Justice believes that it must help build two-
way bridges between labor and the wider community, so that
"working together, we can take our message wherever necessary—
to the board room, city hall, the state legislature, or the Congress."

Since its founding in 1987, JwJ has followed a twofold strategy: to form local chapters and then to coordinate national action.
When Eastern Airlines employees went on strike, Jobs with Justice
organized "drive-throughs"—at coordinated times, hundreds of
cars drove through Eastern hub airports in nearly a dozen cities.
On another occasion, at a prearranged moment, AT&T workers
across the country stood up at their workplaces for five minutes to
call attention to their demand for a fair contract. Not that all JwJ
activities are so dramatic. Some concentrate on careful research—
in 2001, JwJ coalitions issued state-by-state reports in over fifty
cities on job losses attributed to the first seven years of NAFTA.

The bulk of JwJ initiatives, however, are organized by affiliates
acting autonomously. Aware that JwJ coalitions tend to form
around a specific issue and then fade away once that problem is
solved, the Texas organizing committee focuses on building strong
local chapters in four cities—the Dallas-Fort Worth area,
Houston, San Antonio, and Austin. To assure the stability and
continuity of such chapters, JwJ has established a certification
program that requires them to enlist at least five unions and five
community groups as active, dues-paying members. Once that has
been accomplished, chapters can hire their own staff organizers.
Meanwhile, Fetonte is the point person for the state organizing
committee. It's a lot of work, but to him it's not merely an administrative assignment, but a deep personal commitment. Here is
how he describes learning the importance of coalition building:

CWA is one of nine unions that helped found and finance Jobs with Justice nationally, and I've been active in all of our activities for the last fifteen years. I support it because I've seen it work—seen how effective it can be when people come together and actually win.

I learned the value of building coalitions in 1972, when we started a project in East Texas, in Nacogdoches at Stephen F. Austin University. If you applied to work there as an African American, they would circle the "n" in such words as Stephen or Austin at the top of the application [signifying that the applicant was black] and, regardless of your qualifications, you could get a job only in the housekeeping or the food service departments. There was one man who'd been a military policeman for twelve years and had a college degree in political science, but he was given a job as a janitor. The NAACP had been fighting this battle for fifteen years, and even after they finally won in the courts, the university refused to give the workers their back pay.

Finally, in 1983, the NAACP asked for union help. We concentrated on the food service department, where all the workers were black and the supervisors white, and succeeded in organizing the department. So in '85 they announced that they would contract out the entire department! We staged about eight or nine different demonstrations; we went to legislative hearings; we went back to court. Eventually we got the National Labor Relations Board to rule in favor of the union, but what really won for us was the coalition we were able to build. We got the National Organization of Women to join with us, because most of the employees were women. We brought in busloads of demonstrators from Austin, from Houston, from Oklahoma City. And we got both Jesse Jackson and the national president of NOW to come to Nacogdoches. No single local of food service workers could have done that by itself.

Even more importantly, the university employees received local support:

> People put up yard signs. Stores put up signs. A lot of churches got involved. Finally, on December 1, 1987, there was a march of some three thousand people in a town of only about twenty-seven thousand. They started arresting people even though there wasn't any civil disobedience. By now community leaders were urging the university to settle, and eventually we were able to win settlements that included a nine percent wage increase, a grievance procedure, $800,000 in back pay, and preferential hiring for people who'd been discriminated against. As a result there are now black security officers, black librarians. And once we had won that victory, what happened was that other organizing campaigns got going. The service employees were able to start a campaign in nursing homes; the food and commercial workers were able to start one in the chicken plants. By now we had enough support and self-confidence that we could take part in the national campaign against Eastern Airlines.

## An Updated Union Strategy

The lesson of Nacogdoches—that times had changed since the organizing efforts of the 1930s—was not lost on union leadership. As Fetonte explains, the nation's economic structure has changed. Labor used to be able to win its battles when employees put pressure on their employer. But over the last thirty to forty years, corporations merged and consolidated and multinationals bought out local and regional companies. If one local goes on strike the owners are quite willing to take a loss at that particular branch or even close it down. "When CWA organized MCI workers in a suburb of Detroit," Fetonte says, "we signed up three hundred of the four hundred people who worked there. We filed the Labor Board petition on a Friday. On Sunday they closed the place down."

Texas presents a particular challenge. According to Anannya Bhattacherjee, the former Veatch program officer who recommended a grant to Texas Jobs with Justice,

> Workers and their communities face enormous barriers to building power in Texas. When workers try to build organizations they often face aggressive attacks. Eight in ten employers hire consultants to advise them on how to defeat workers' organizing efforts; half the employers threaten to shut down if workers organize; and over three in ten fire workers who are active in organizing. All this adds up to conditions where working families are not able to earn a living wage, have access to health care, or live in safe and affordable communities.

To make matters worse, thousands of Texas workers lost their jobs between 1994 and 2000 and only 2.5 percent of the workforce now belongs to unions. To make things still worse, the federal government has turned actively antilabor. Under the Reagan and first Bush Administrations, the health and safety inspectors were replaced with auditors to go after unions. Under the second Bush Administration the situation is deteriorating even further. As a result, says Fetonte, "Wages are going down, health benefits are going down, and safety violations have gone through the roof. CWA is the sixth or fifth-largest union in the country, but even we no longer have the power to fight these battles on our own." In response, the union now asks its members to sign pledge cards promising to support somebody else's fight at least five times a year—and hopes that other organizations will reciprocate. "If all of us are willing to stand up for other people's rights, then eventually we can start winning again," Fetonte sums up.

The Bush Administration is also threatening the job security of federal workers by privatizing government functions such as those of the US Postal Service, and by changing state subsidies for specific functions to block grants. For example, when the federal government gives money to states for unemployment insurance or job training, the law dictates that the people hired to carry out these functions must be civil servants or their equivalent, but once states pay for these programs out of their own budgets, even if supplemented by block grants, the federal guarantee no longer applies. The legislation setting up the Department of Homeland Security may serve as a precedent for this trend.

Meanwhile, Fetonte stresses, JwJ is beginning to win some important battles despite such hostility and economic trends:

> The thing is that you can't expect to win overnight. Take one of our most recent victories, the fight to get a decent contract for Tejano [Mexican] musicians in San Antonio, providing for parity with "Anglo" musicians. That effort was led by San Antonio Jobs with Justice, and again it was a strong cooperative effort, with the Latin music director of the American Federation of Musicians and Rudy Anderson, our state organizer, playing major roles. Now our goal is to hire a full-time organizer in San Antonio and the Veatch grant is a big help in our ability to staff up. The problem up to now has been that Texas JwJ has tried to function with people like me who already have full-time jobs, so for continuity Jobs with Justice needs its own full-time organizers in each of the four major Texas cities.
>
> The way Rudy Anderson came to us is interesting and illustrates what's going on. Rudy was president of his local in an AT&T plant in Mesquite, a suburb of Dallas. Then that company was spun off as part of Lucent, and most recently it was owned by Tyco. Then Tyco closed it down. That, by the way, was the last telephone manufacturing plant in the United States—they've all gone offshore.

One of the reasons it's so hard to protect workers' rights, according to Fetonte, is the difference in attitude between the two major political parties:

> Every time the Republicans move in, they use the power of appointment to control the National Labor Relations Board

and all the regional boards. At the time Clinton got elected, every one of the regional directors was a former labor attorney who'd been representing the employers, but Clinton didn't remove them. Then, I think in '92 or '93, there was a really bad NLRB ruling against the clothing workers union and we organized demonstrations and sit-ins at board headquarters and the regional boards. Jesse Jackson got arrested and so did three union international vice presidents. I think it took thirty-five sit-ins before we got Clinton to move. Now the Republicans are back in power and all the boards that are supposed to protect workers are once again being stacked against them.

Fetonte believes that the government's antilabor policies are not only hurting working people but the country as a whole. He explains,

From the thirties to the early seventies, labor unions were really able to improve people's lives, and that's what created the middle class that is the foundation of our economy. The public doesn't seem to understand that the strength of the middle class was based on justice where people work. Now that base is being steadily eroded. It's a matter of raw power, and very few corporations deal with labor in an ethical, decent way. I think they're making a mistake, because the economic health of this country depends on people's ability to buy their products, and that is being deliberately destroyed.

Yet when unions struggle for decent jobs and wages, a large part of the public perceives it as a selfish fight just for their own personal benefit. On the other hand, when community and advocacy groups fight without allies, they rarely have the power to prevail. Therefore, the basic strategy of Jobs with Justice is to form union and community coalitions designed to outlast specific issues and initiatives.

The key words, over and over, are *coalition* and *continuity*. Russ Davis, director of Massachusetts Jobs with Justice, made the same point at the 2003 UUA General Assembly. In Boston, he reports, JwJ was instrumental in forming a coalition in support of Boston janitors who were striking for decent wages, healthcare, and full-time jobs. The coalition marched and rallied and built support in diverse communities. "The strike was an important first step, but much work remains to be done." Davis continues,

> These are tough times we're facing. The Bush administration is waging a war on workers. . . . Many of us are facing layoffs and the loss of our healthcare. Immigrant rights, civil liberties, and our right to organize unions are threatened by draconian laws like the USA Patriot Act. We need to stand together as never before.
>
> But the movement to support the janitors showed that another vision based on solidarity, not corporate greed, is possible.

Such successes require permanent staffing, which in turn requires money. Two Veatch grants of $30,000 each went to JwJ in Texas and Massachusetts in 2003; in St. Louis the Veatch visitors were told that a similar grant was critical in enabling JwJ to maintain an office and a paid director. Nor is the national Jobs with Justice Education Fund neglected; its efforts to develop a national network of affiliates have been supported by a grant of $75,000. Thus the spirit of Caroline Veatch and the vision of the Veatch Program's pioneers live on.

# Interfaith Worker Justice
## *Enlisting the Religious Community*

As PART OF its mission to build broad coalitions between grassroots organizations, the Veatch Program helps to support not only Jobs with Justice but also an organization with similar objectives, Interfaith Worker Justice (IWJ). One of the Interfaith group's 2003 priorities was passage of a federal Fair Minimum Wage Act. Kim Bobo, executive director, points out that anyone working a forty-hour week at the current minimum wage earns a bare $10,700 a year—almost $5,000 under the poverty line for a family of three. In fact, adjusted for inflation, today's minimum wage is worth 24 cents less than it was in 1979. The act would have raised the minimum wage by $1.50 an hour to $6.65 over a fourteen-month period, Bobo says. "That's certainly not as high as it needs to go, but for workers who make the minimum wage it's a big deal, and I think it's critical that we not lose sight of economic justice issues." Even this meager increase did not pass. In any case, she explains, even if it had passed, there would have been a serious loophole:

> The Bush Administration pushed an amendment that would allow states to opt out of the increase. That is a ridiculous proposal. It's a proposal that completely undermines the idea of having a minimum wage, and I think it's part of the

fact that this government is engaged in an assault on workers, and trying to do it in a way that people won't notice.

More than twenty national religious leaders signed the committee's petition on behalf of the Fair Minimum Wage Act, including Rev. William Sinkford, president of the Unitarian Universalist Association; Denise Moorehead, representing the UU Service Committee; the president of the Disciples of Christ; the stated clerk of the Presbyterian Church (USA) General Assembly; and the general secretary of the National Council of Churches.

Another issue that leads Bobo to suspect the Bush Administration of being engaged in an assault on working people is that Secretary of Labor Elaine Chao has proposed weakening the law that established overtime regulations and the forty-hour work week. Bobo says,

> This law has been in force since 1938, but Secretary Chao, who is as unfriendly to labor as anyone can be, weakened it by proposing that instead of being entitled to overtime pay for working more than forty hours in a single week, you'd get overtime only if you've worked more than eighty hours in a two-week period. And she did that by Administrative action rather than asking Congress to change the law. In other words, the Administration is trying to undo seventy years of protection, and doing it without anyone paying attention. This is going to be an uphill battle, but it is such a fundamental battle that we'll be fighting as hard as we can. We'll be mobilizing the religious community and seeking the help of other key organizations. We feel morally compelled to play a leadership role on this issue because, unfortunately, there are not lots of other people out there who seem to care.

According to the Labor Department, only 100,000 workers would lose their protection as a result of this change; critics however say the number is closer to six million. An unusual bipartisan coalition in Congress is trying to overturn Chao's action, but in the face of a veto threat by the president, the outcome is uncertain.

These are not the only battles Interfaith Worker Justice is fighting, and Kim Bobo's tenacious commitment and the upbeat, sparkling personality that keeps her from getting discouraged are equally impressive. Having spent some ten years working for Bread for the World, a church-based antihunger group, Bobo went on to become the founder of Interfaith Worker Justice (then called the Interfaith Committee for Worker Justice) in 1996. "It became obvious to me," she says, "that the religious community had to be more involved with labor issues. It seemed obvious that you can't just support shelters and soup kitchens—that you have to deal with economic justice."

This premise so clearly coincides with the basic principles of the Veatch Program that it is no surprise that Veatch grants support not only the national organization but also some of its sixty local affiliates.

## Abolishing Sweat Shops

As Rabbi Robert J. Marx, the board president of Interfaith Worker Justice, says,

> Amid the heat of industrial laundries, along the floors of poultry plant factories, within the crowded conditions of the nation's nursing homes, Interfaith Worker Justice has provided a ringing, prophetic voice for workers, and their rights and dignity on the job.

Helping sweatshop workers takes special effort because many of them are immigrants unsure of their rights, and if they are undocumented, they feel particularly vulnerable. One such immigrant worker, Ricardo Veisaga, speaks from personal experience:

> Once I left my home country, I fell victim to an organized mafia dedicated to exploiting human beings. I was made to work twelve to fourteen hours a day, seven days a week. I slept on a floor with no blankets and was locked in my room throughout the night. After escaping, I connected with the

Chicago Interfaith Committee, which helped me file a claim
for back wages and connected me with legal services. So
many people in this country have no clue as to the abuses
immigrant workers face. Interfaith Worker Justice brings
these abuses to light.

The organization works closely with labor unions to prevent
such exploitation, and one recent example was the drive to organize poultry workers. Unfortunately, the organizing effort did not
produce quick results and a lot of the unions backed off. After all,
many of them feel that their primary responsibility is to their own
members; that organizing the unorganized is a secondary priority.
But IWJ feels it has a moral responsibility not to give up. "We feel
that if we start something we can't just drop it," Bobo explained.
Because Department of Labor staff refused to meet with a worker-
led delegation, IWJ mobilized 150 clergy and community leaders
to sign an open letter to Secretary Chao in support of poultry
workers' right to back wages. Finally, in June of 2001, Chao agreed
to meet with a delegation, led by Kim Bobo, of seventeen clergy
members, attorneys, and worker's rights advocates. It was the
beginning of a prolonged effort. In Bobo's words,

> We had to get out hundreds of letters to the secretary and her
> staff, and eventually we pushed the department to investi-
> gate the industry and then to hold it accountable for paying
> people. We realized that Secretary Chao is very antilabor, but
> we also realize that there are two groups the administration
> seems to care about: Latinos and Catholics. They consider
> them swing voters. So we enlisted the help of Latino groups
> and Catholic bishops, and we actually got the DOL to move
> a little bit. And despite Chao's attitude, some of the local
> inspectors and regional administrators are absolutely fabu-
> lous. They have a real commitment to workers and they
> cheer us on.

When more than four thousand poultry workers filed suit for
back wages, local interfaith committees distributed bulletins in

congregations near poultry plants, asking for their help. The workers eventually received $10 million in back pay, with many millions more due in the future. Bobo says of this triumph, "Those close to the Department of Labor confirm that the settlement would not have occurred without our persistence."

An issue of the committee's newsletter, *Faith Works*, reports on other successes. In Chicago, seven thousand low-wage hotel workers received a contract that gave them a significant raise, more affordable health insurance, and protection against unreasonable work loads. "The religious community's involvement was absolutely crucial to this victory," the story comments. For instance, Chicago IWJ held training sessions for hotel workers showing them how they could get their clergy involved in the campaign. "Many workers were inspired by the possibility of bringing together two important parts of their lives: their faith and their struggle for justice in the workplace," reads the article. IWJ volunteers also joined thousands of workers in a march down Michigan Avenue during rush hour and helped to obtain a letter of support from Cardinal Francis George.

In Boston, meanwhile, IWJ helped recruit religious support for striking janitors. Clergy members, including Rev. John Gilmore of Unitarian Universalists for a Just Economic Community, held vigils outside the offices of cleaning contractors, attended negotiating sessions, and participated in a "Labor in the Pulpits" program that resulted in more than twenty congregations inviting janitors to speak to their members.

The headline of another story in *Faith Works* reads, "Unitarians Endorse Pickles Boycott." According to the story,

> The Unitarian Universalist Service Committee (UUSC) joined hundreds of churches, labor unions, and social justice organizations nationwide who have endorsed the Farm Labor Organizing Committee's national boycott of Mt. Olive Pickles. Called in 1999 in protest of working conditions in eastern North Carolina farm fields where Mt. Olive procures its cucumbers, the farm worker supporters have pledged to

continue the boycott until Mt. Olive Co. gives farm workers
a direct voice concerning working conditions.*

Interfaith Worker Justice is waging an even tougher battle to
improve the abysmal working conditions of laundry workers. In
support of their uphill struggle to organize, IWJ and its affiliates
in eight priority areas seek to establish religious support committees which, as Kim Bobo explains, "don't directly support the
organizing effort, but they seek to protect the workers' right to do
it. It's a matter of mobilizing the religious community to put a wall
of protection around the workers, so they don't get fired or
harassed" for trying to organize.

## Working with Government Agencies

While the main objective of Interfaith Worker Justice remains the
building of partnerships between the labor movement and the
religious community, it recently became apparent that this isn't
enough—that obtaining justice for workers also requires a partnership between the religious community and government agencies, especially those that are supposed to be protecting workers'
rights. As Bobo explains,

> We came to realize that working with the Department of
> Labor and state departments of labor is really important at
> this moment in our history. For one thing, 85 percent of
> workers are not unionized. Unfortunately, that includes
> huge numbers of low-wage immigrant workers, who some-
> times don't even get paid the money they have earned. We
> try to help people by creating worker centers and worker
> counseling programs. We have had some success helping
> workers to file complaints and in some cases getting back
> wages they are owed and other settlements.

---

* As this book was going to press, the Mt. Olive Pickle company announced that it had
signed a contract with the Farm Labor Organizing Committee, ending the boycott. An
unusual provision of the settlement is that it calls for a union hiring hall in Mexico to
recruit guest workers.

In Miami, IWJ has worked out an agreement with the Wage and Hours Division of the local Department of Labor. Bobo explains, "Under that agreement, when the religious community identifies a bad workplace situation, they go tell the owner that the Department of Labor will be in the next day to inspect." The Unitarian Universalist Congregation of Miami has been heavily engaged in this effort. Regarding her congregation's role, Rev. Lucy Hitchcock Seck says,

> We held two conferences in 2003 cosponsored with the South Florida Interfaith Committee for Worker Justice to encourage other congregations to become informed about worker justice issues. By the way, there is a strong Veatch connection: The South Florida committee is a Veatch grantee, and we received funding from the UU Fund for Social Responsibility, which in turn is supported by Veatch.
>
> We sent out some 1,600 invitations, which pointed out that, according to the U.S. Census, Miami is the poorest city in the nation, and while American workers enjoy many rights and protections, too often laws are not enforced or working people are unaware of the rights to which they are entitled. Frankly, we were somewhat disappointed that only about fifty congregations participated. At the first workshop, with Kim Bobo as one of the speakers, we introduced a worker rights manual the Interfaith Committee had prepared, which shows faith communities how to set up counseling services for low-wage workers. The second workshop offered specific training on the use of the manual and focused on making faith communities effective advocates for the rights of the poor. The aim of both workshops was to educate ourselves and our religious communities about the urgent situation of the working poor, and to involve the faith community in proactive solutions to the plight of the working poor in our community.

A third conference is being planned to reach out to evangelical congregations, since they are the most likely to have minority group memberships.

One of the most vulnerable groups in the Miami area are the homeless, many of whom are hired by the day to do agricultural labor. "After they get picked up to work," Hitchcock Seck reports, "they then get charged for transportation and for lunch, so at the end of the day they get paid almost nothing. Our program seeks to raise their awareness of their rights." When they have a complaint, they can notify any of the cooperating congregations, which will then help them to get satisfaction. Depending on the circumstances, the volunteer advocate will then contact the employer, turn the complaint over to a government agency, file a small claims case, or, if it is a collective problem, get union help. Staff assistance and further training are available if needed.

The fact that the Unitarian Universalist church is so heavily involved in this effort is no coincidence, Hitchcock Seck explains,

> When the UU Fund for Social Responsibility gave its grant to the South Florida Interfaith Committee for Worker Justice they included a provision requiring them to work with a local UU congregation. We're very grateful for that because it helped to put us on the map in the social justice arena after many years of our not being very much involved.

Nationally, IWJ includes a board representative from UUs for a Just Economic Environment. At the time of this interview Kim Bobo was looking for one more. "Representation is roughly proportional," she explains, "so we have about ten Catholics on our board, and the next largest representation are probably the Methodists, but we are looking for ways to strengthen our ties with the Unitarian Universalists because, while a small denomination, they are disproportionately active."

In that connection, she stresses the importance of Veatch support: "We use their grants for general support, because you can't do the core work, such as building affiliated groups around the country, without it. And that's the hardest money to get, so we greatly appreciate the help we get from the Veatch Program."

Like so many grant recipients, Bobo stresses the personal relationship with the Veatch staff:

I can tell you, as somebody who has to raise the money, not all funding sources are the same. Maybe it's because in larger organizations the staff handles so many requests that they develop an attitude that you're trying to take away their money; whatever the reason, that's never been true at Veatch. Their staff has always been tremendously interested in our work, supportive of our work, and respectful of us as people.

This is not to suggest, of course, that other denominations are not also supportive. Lately, Interfaith Worker Justice has made an effort to reach out to Mormons and to members of the Islamic community. In 2002 it held its first Islam and Labor Conference in Chicago. Thus different faith communities are discovering that the bonds that unite them may be more important than their theological differences. As Bruce Jay, coordinator of the South Florida committee, puts it, "Honoring the worth and dignity of every person is a concept that can unite us in a common cause, since it is the basis of all our faith traditions."

## Seminary Summer

Some recent reports indicate that young men now entering the Catholic priesthood are more conservative (both theologically and politically) than in previous generations. At the same time, the mainline Protestant denominations are losing influence, while evangelicals, who are often hard-right, are gaining power. But Bobo is not ready to give up. Realizing that it only takes a handful of dedicated clergy members to keep up the momentum of interfaith work, her organization has set up a program to identify and train the leaders of the future.

Called Seminary Summer, the program brings interns from various faith groups to "plan, pray, and protest for worker justice." In 2002, twenty-eight interns from ten faith traditions enrolled in the program; over the last few years more than one hundred have participated. One of them, Joey Mokos, a recent graduate of Yale Divinity School, recalls what it was like:

The program ran ten weeks. Week one was devoted to orientation in Chicago; then for about the next nine weeks we were placed all over with labor unions, central labor councils, or interfaith organizations. After that, we went back to Chicago for debriefing—sharing our experiences, learning from each other. That was terrifically exciting.

My placement was in New Haven with the Federation of Hospital and University Employees, spending one week each with three different unions, and then one week with the Connecticut Center for a New Economy.

Mokos put his lessons and commitment literally on the line—the picket line—during the Yale strike in early 2003. Serving as a picket captain, "I would show up first thing in the morning to sign people in and give them directions as to where they were needed." Then he started looking for a job as either a labor or community organizer. Why not the priesthood? "Well," he says, sounding a bit bemused, "I got married." The story of the Yale struggle continues in the next chapter.

# Connecticut Center for
# a New Economy
## *Developing a Social Contract for New Haven*

THE ORGANIZATION Joe Mokos worked for as an intern is the Connecticut Center for a New Economy (CCNE). Connecticut, with the highest per capita income in the nation, might not seem like a state in need of grassroots organizing on behalf of workplace justice. But it also has some other distinctions. In the past decade, Connecticut has experienced the country's greatest increase in working poverty, with nearly 12 percent of its children now living below the official poverty line. And while it is the home of Yale University, whose $11 million endowment is one of the largest in the nation, Yale's home city of New Haven is one of the ten poorest in the United States.

Twice in 2003, these glaring contradictions led some two thousand protesters to take to the streets to demonstrate their solidarity with the Yale janitors, secretaries, dining hall workers, and graduate teaching assistants when they went on strike against the university. As the *New York Times* described the scene, "Defying bitter cold and stinging gusts of wind, the strikers crowded Yale's sidewalks and picketed in front of its austere stone buildings." Even Yale's president,

Richard C. Levin, concedes, "I think that historically Yale has not been the most supportive employer. We can do better, and we have done better in the last decade." But not well enough to satisfy its workers.

One of the demonstrators and organizers was Lyndon Pitter, president of New Haven's Jamaican American Movement, and a board member of the CCNE. In addition to pay and pensions, a major union goal was to win recognition at Yale-New Haven Hospital. Pitter explains the group's tactics this way:

> The key thing in this kind of struggle is to make sure that the workers understand that there is tremendous support for them in the larger community. . . . That's why we worked hard to turn out a crowd that included not only workers but African Americans, Caucasians, Hispanics, clergy—a wide spectrum of people from all walks of life. Even some students participated.

This was not the first time Yale workers had gone on strike; there were two in 1996, five others going back to 1968. One of the 1996 strikes led to the founding of the Connecticut Center for a New Economy. The catalyst was Andrea Cole, now CCNE's executive director.

Born in South Africa, Cole had been active in antiapartheid efforts and came to the United States because "I needed to get my children out so they wouldn't have to grow up under [that] system." She brought with her a determination not to put up with injustice of any kind. She points out that Yale is the city's largest employer, and recalls,

> In 1996, Yale tried to eliminate six hundred good union jobs, and the people in those jobs were primarily African American residents, living in some of the most disadvantaged neighborhoods of New Haven. I was a secretary in Yale's economics department and got involved in the attempts to organize a union of Yale clerical workers. I became a union leader, and

every time there was a strike, I was the person who had to go out into the community to ask for support.

Thus she found herself becoming, almost by default, a community organizer:

> We were able to fend of Yale's efforts to destroy these jobs, and in the process I started to work with a number of people from the community. The unions then decided that there needed to be one union person responsible for community organizing, and I was that person.

Cole began by maintaining the coalition she had built and to enlist it in objectives beyond the immediate issue of jobs at Yale. One of her earliest priorities was to work for city legislation guaranteeing a living wage. Then came an opportunity to demonstrate the power of the coalition. A major hotel went bankrupt and the city voted to give $10 million to redevelop it. The coalition said: *Stop. If you're going to give public money for a private enterprise, you need to insist on employment standards so people will earn a living wage.* While the coalition won this battle, it also demonstrated to Cole the need for a more permanent, more powerful organization: "So along with a couple of other people I decided to form a non-profit organization."

Incorporated in 1999, CCNE began to raise money locally, but its ambitious objectives called for more secure and more substantial sources of income. As it happened, one of the other founders was a former Veatch program officer, and she suggested applying to the Veatch Program for a grant. Cole says that made all the difference. "Their grant enabled me to hire as a lead organizer an African American pastor who had been a community leader for a long time but had never had the opportunity to develop his leadership and organizing skills." Starting with ten grassroots leaders in New Haven, CCNE now has more than sixty leaders statewide, "and each of those sixty," according to Cole, "is now speaking to additional leaders and getting more people excited about the program."

Lyndon Pitter has been one such leader from the beginning. He explains,

> I was cochair of one of the organizing groups [in the Omni Hotel strike]. When the strike started, our neighborhood organization formed an alliance with the union, because we felt that one way to improve the quality of life for residents was to make sure that their rights are respected and that they have secure jobs. That's how I got to know Andrea Cole, and I've been active with CCNE ever since.

> When the Yale workers went on strike, CCNE again spearheaded the community organizing effort. It's an effort to bring the unions and the churches and the public together to arrive at a common agenda. We call that agenda the Social Contract. It represents the concerns of workers, of ordinary folks, of the wider community. The next step is to promote an agenda that shows people—working people, parents, just about everyone in the community—that they have a stake in developments in their neighborhood and their city. That's the key role of CCNE: we are the keepers of the Social Contract to make sure it becomes a living reality.

## Confronting the Statewide Problem

As president and catalyst of the organization, Andrea Cole confirms its basic objectives and strategies:

> What distinguishes our group from many others is our concept of organizing. What we are attempting to build is a broad-based movement around the issues of economic and social change. We began by building a model in New Haven, and then letting that model be utilized in other areas of the state.

> Many other organizations tend to organize around a single issue: housing or public education or jobs. Our model calls, first of all, for identifying common issues, and then forming

a network to develop a common agenda that deals with the day-to-day lives of working families. Such an agenda would, for instance, include the ability to get good jobs and the right to have a voice on the job, plus good housing, really good public education, and health care for all.

That's one focus—working together. Our other focus is developing leadership and teaching organizing skills—to get more people involved and show them how to achieve a better society. That's why, in addition to one-on-one training, we run leadership training sessions every six to eight weeks.

One of the first communities where the New Haven model was applied was the nearby city of Stamford, where the powers-that-be were about to demolish two units of public housing. "We managed to prevent that," Cole says, "by organizing people in the community, getting the churches involved, marching, and attending council meetings." They did even better than preventing the demolition: They got the city council to pass an ordinance that requires the city to replace every unit of public housing that's demolished with a new one.

Next they tackled the state Department of Motor Vehicles, which had drafted restrictive regulations that would have made it difficult for immigrants to obtain driver licenses:

We were instrumental in getting the department to drop these regulations, which would have imposed an enormous burden on immigrants who had certain kinds of visas or had visas pending. We sent busloads of immigrants to public hearings, and recruited a number of religious and community leaders who were very outspoken on the issue.

We have also shifted the debate about public education in New Haven, which is now spreading across the state. We brought in two national leaders who had revolutionized public education in Tennessee to explain how to reduce class size, and we engaged the board of education, the public, and the city government in the debate about public education. The issue is how do you prepare young people today for better jobs and better quality of life, so they don't wind up washing dishes and mopping floors?

Nothing illustrates this need better than New Haven's experience with Science Park. When manufacturing jobs disappeared from Connecticut in the 1970s and 1980s, New Haven alone lost 20,000 jobs. The hope was that biotechnology would fill the gap. Science Park was founded in 1981 as a high-tech incubator of new jobs, and in 1982 it succeeded in attracting its first medical research start-up.

Twenty years later, CCNE studied the results and found that only four hundred biotechnology jobs had been created, that despite generous tax credits and other subsidies only a single company remained—and that this sole survivor was planning to move.

Why?

As the *New Haven Register* reported, "The severe shortage of skilled technical workers is of statewide and national concern, but community leaders say solving the problem is crucial for New Haven if it wants to court high-tech companies and keep them in town." This shortage exists even though the local community college offered a one-year biotechnology certificate program in an attempt to train local residents for such jobs. William Battle was among those who tried hard to recruit students, describing it as a "massive effort." But then he received a fax from the person in charge of the program. "'Mr. Battle, we have a problem," the fax said. "The kids that are applying for the course can't pass English and Math 100."

Meanwhile, Yale receives millions in research grants, licensing fees, and royalty payments from biotechnology companies. As part of its agenda to promote a new economy, CCNE is urging Yale to find ways to encourage biotechnology companies to settle and *stay* in New Haven . . . and to make substantial payments to improve New

Haven's public schools. But as Andrea Cole says in discussing what it takes to develop a new social contract, "It's going to take time."

To speed the process, the organization has taken to publishing carefully researched, clearly written and designed brochures on such issues as jobs and education. For instance, a brochure called "Good Jobs, Strong Communities" says in its introduction,

> Manufacturing jobs became good jobs in the middle of the twentieth century when workers by the millions organized themselves into unions and bargained high wages, good benefits and job security. Millions of service sector workers could do the same thing with the same effect. Some argue that service employers can't afford high wages, but thousands of service sector employees work for large, profitable employers.... [This publication] examines the historic shift in Connecticut's economy, and illuminates policy options for improving wages. In particular, the report focuses on the role of unionization—one of the most effective tools for raising wages and one of the most often ignored policy options—in setting community standards for good jobs.

Through careful, dispassionate analysis the report then documents these concepts.

"Our reports capture public attention," says Lyndon Pitter. "They bring the message to the people so they become better informed citizens and better informed voters, and they also inform public officials. Then we follow up the facts with action. These reports become living instruments of change."

This facts-and-action model has succeeded in getting a number of living wage ordinances passed not only in New Haven but in other jurisdictions. It has also managed to obtain what are called "card check" agreements, under which employers and employees agree to let workers achieve union recognition once a majority signs union authorization cards.

The report also explores the national dimension of the problem by detailing the failure of American universities to prepare a diverse workforce capable of meeting the nation's need for economic growth. The report quotes Yale president Levin as saying: "By reaching out to ensure that we bring into our student body and into our workforce women and individuals of underrepresented minority groups, we aid the University in achieving its mission and benefit the nation as well." And in fact, in 2000, around 30 percent of Yale's bachelor degrees went to members of minority groups. Laudable as that may be, African Americans and Latinos together still make up 54 percent of Yale's service and maintenance staff and, CCNE claims, current hiring practices keep minorities in lower-wage, entry-level jobs. Adding a personal perspective, Michael López says, "I took a test ten years ago and qualified to enter the trades helper program, but Yale never followed through. I never got the training. If I had, I'd be in a top job now instead of stuck in the middle."

## Shifting the Dynamics of Power

So is the glass half empty or half full?

Undoubtedly, the Connecticut Center for a New Economy has, in a remarkably short time, been successful in recruiting faith-based organizations, labor unions, civil rights organizations, and immigrant advocacy groups in its efforts to achieve a social contract. One notable recent victory was a vote by the New Haven city council to revoke the arresting power of the Yale-New Haven Hospital police. Before that, Pitter points out, "they would arrest workers who were passing out union leaflets. We got the council to put this item on their agenda, and several debates and public hearings later, they finally voted to revoke the arresting power."

The CCNE can also take credit for convincing the state attorney general to file suit against the hospital to make it account for its use of the "free bed fund." This is federal/state money to reimburse hospitals for taking care of the uninsured, but a CCNE report pointed out that the hospital was using the fund for general operating expenses. Contrasting with his gentle Island accent, Pitter says bitterly, "they have a huge endowment but they want to live on just the interest. They put profits before patients; profits before people."

Andrea Cole describes another important but less observable CCNE achievement. It has made people who struggle to make a living more aware of the reasons why they have trouble making ends meet:

> When people understand their situations, it makes a very profound difference. For example, they may be working two or three jobs to pay the rent, and still their debts exceed their income. Because of the way it's depicted in the media, most of them feel that they personally have failed. When we're able to show them that actually there is a structural shift that has happened that has put them in this position, it's very liberating.
>
> It's motivating for grassroots people who are struggling to survive to know what creates these situations and that they have the power to change things. Once they know the facts about the local and national economy, when they attend a public hearing on reducing class size, for example, they understand how this problem fits into the larger picture

Veatch funding, she says, is instrumental in making these achievements possible:

> Veatch plays an extraordinary role in funding work that is not just about charity but is about real social change. There are some people who think that social justice work means giving to the poor and running soup kitchens. Those are good things, but what we're trying to do is to fundamentally shift the dynamics of power, and the courage of Veatch is being willing to support this effort. The ultimate objective is to help ordinary working people to bring about change so their own quality of life can be benefited.

Board member Pitter, chuckling at his understatement, says, "For the kind of work we're doing, bringing attention to the issues that affect workers and ordinary citizens, well, you don't get corporate funding for that." That is why organizations like his turn to the Veatch Program for support. And Veatch is not unaware of how controversial such backing can be. There is a poster in one of the program officers' offices with this quote by Dom Helder Camara: "When I gave food to the poor they called me a saint. When I ask why the poor have no food, they call me a communist."

Yes, Veatch, too, has had its share of critics. There are always those who see any attempt to cure the faults in our economic or political system as an example—to use a phrase currently popular with those defending their privileged positions—of class warfare. If it is indeed a war, we can only hope that the good guys win.

# Alabama Arise
## *Organizing for Justice*

IF BEING POOR in Connecticut is tough, being poor and black in Alabama has to be even harder. But in Alabama, as in Connecticut, success in attaining justice begins with a sense of solidarity, and so it is encouraging that Alabama Arise enjoys a strong sense of ownership of its members. "They call Arise 'us,' not 'you,'" says Kimble Forrister, the organization's executive director.

The sentiment is echoed by Helen Hamilton Rivas, an active volunteer. "People interested in justice are good folks, good to be with," she says. "And they have a sense of humor. They've got to in order to survive!" Those who work with Alabama Arise have achieved this kind of long-haul commitment on the part of both its types of volunteers—the poor who stand to gain a personal benefit and the more affluent activists who support them.

Organizing a community for social justice is never fast or easy, and it is particularly challenging when the goal is to organize an entire state. As Alabama Arise said in its application for a Veatch grant,

> Organizing for change in state policies requires a statewide strategy. We cannot achieve substantial wins by organizing only the poor, or only African Americans, or only a few neighborhoods. We were able to change the conversation on welfare reform by first listening to low-income people and determining

an authentic advocacy message, but then organizing in suburban Republican districts as well. . . . Through Arise's extensive network of members, our 'citizen lobbyists' make their
views known to their elected representatives. In both rural
and urban swing districts we focus our efforts on equipping
citizens with the knowledge and tools to speak to their legislators effectively.

## Focus on the Legislature

Launched in 1988, with thirty-two member groups, Arise now has
some 150 affiliates and is supported by dues from both organizational and individual members, as well as by grants, such as the
Veatch Program's support of the Arise Citizens' Policy Project,
which backs up Arise through research and public education,
using fact sheets, media relations, and meetings. The dues are
critical not only for the money they raise but also as a sign of commitment. In fact, one of the Veatch criteria for its grants is that the
grant recipient must have a base of grassroots support to demonstrate member loyalty. Equally important as expressions of loyalty,
according to Forrister, are commitments of time in organizing
local meetings, writing letters to the editor, phoning legislators, or
visiting the statehouse during the legislature's biennial meetings.
The legislative effort usually begins with a "Kick-Off" day in
January, when Arise announces its agenda and provides a forum
for the citizens most directly affected by the issues. In 2003, the
priorities were two bills the organization had drafted, one dealing
with tenants' rights, the other with payday loans. "We also worked
with three tax reform coalitions to prepare for a special session on
tax reform," says Forrister.

In a typical year, approximately two hundred volunteers
swarm over the state capitol, meeting with as many as ninety legislators for a preview briefing, followed by lunch with some forty of
them. Rev. Dana Jordan Allende, minister of the Auburn Unitarian
Universalist Fellowship, reported after attending a kick-off meeting

that the preparatory training helps to "equip ordinary citizens with basic presentation skills and to demystify the political process." Writing in her congregational newsletter she continues,

> One of the most startling discoveries I made was to learn that in many (if not most) cases, well-informed citizens may know more about a particular issue than their legislators. In fact, senators and representatives depend upon groups such as Alabama Arise to provide them background information. A recent newspaper article quoted one representative who admitted that although he doesn't always support the Alabama Arise position, he nevertheless appreciates and relies upon the thoroughness and accuracy of the information they provide. The thing that really gladdened my heart was being with a diverse group of concerned and committed people joining forces for common cause. We were young and old, black and white, Methodist, Catholic, Lutheran, Unitarian, and Holiness . . . with a range of income levels.

Like Rivas, Allende stresses that "folks with a peace and justice perspective are good company," and added that "this work provides a much needed antidote to our feelings of political powerlessness and inordinate concern for our own well-being."

The Auburn Fellowship is one of five Unitarian Universalist congregations that support the Arise effort. It is, says Allende, "an affiliation of which we can be proud."

Explaining that the top legislative objectives are established not by the staff or by the board but by the members, Forrister describes the process:

> Arise works hard to be an authentic voice of the community. Through summer listening sessions in communities around the state, half with low-income groups, members provide input on proposed policy priorities. At the September annual meeting, the member groups consider the input from the listening sessions and the political viability of the proposals, and then choose their legislative agenda for the coming year by a

process of cumulative voting. In 2002, the members chose to work on tax reform, constitution reform, public transportation, landlord-tenant law, child care, predatory lending, and a moratorium on executions.

Helen Rivas, as a member of two groups that support Arise—the Birmingham Unitarian Church and Centro Cultural Latino—participated in several listening sessions, which she describes as "very relaxed":

> At our church we have scheduled them between our two Sunday morning services and during our family night. They usually start with an Arise organizer explaining the issues that were chosen the previous year, and mentioning additional issues suggested at other listening sessions. For instance, Centro Cultural got Arise to support letting immigrants obtain driver's licenses with documents other than their Social Security numbers.
>
> After the explanations and discussion, the group votes on its priorities, and all the results then get pooled and tabulated.

The Arise priorities make up a far-reaching and challenging list, but then Alabama has the dubious distinction of providing some of the most challenging social justice problems. For instance, Alabama has the lowest funding in the nation for social services and a notoriously unfair tax policy. As the Episcopal bishop of Alabama said at a joint press conference of religious leaders: "Our taxation policy in Alabama places an undue burden on the poorest of our citizens." What's more, he went on, "Tax revenues are not adequate to fund our schools and provide critical preschool and early childhood opportunities."

Could this be the way in which Alabama becomes the model for the nation at large?

In fact, the tax laws in Alabama are so egregiously unfair that Arise has enlisted potent support from religious groups and four of the state's leading newspapers for its efforts to reform them. In the 2002 gubernatorial election, both major party candidates responded to an Arise questionnaire with a promise of reform, and the winning Republican candidate said: "I believe it is absolutely immoral that we charge an income tax on someone who makes $4,600 a year." He actually managed to get tax reform on the ballot, but the voters turned it down.

Nathan Morgan, an Arise policy analyst, spells out the details:

> Alabama has one of the most regressive tax systems in the country. The poorest Alabamians pay three times as much of their income in state and local taxes as do the richest. In effect, we tax poor people deeper into poverty in Alabama.

Consider two examples:

- Joe is a full-time worker. With an income less than $20,000, his family is among the poorest fifth in Alabama. Families in his income group pay, on average, 11.5 cents in state and local taxes on every dollar they make.

- George, on the other hand, is extremely wealthy. With an income over $243,000, his family is among the richest 1 percent of Alabamians. Families in his income group pay, on average, 3.6 cents in state and local taxes on every dollar they make.

Morgan adds, "Baby formula is taxed in Alabama but calf feed is not. Why do baby cows rate a tax break and not baby humans? Laundry detergent is subject to a sales tax, but dry cleaning is not, so low-income families pay a sales tax to wash their clothes, while wealthier families get their clothes dry-cleaned tax free."

Morgan says he believes that this truly bizarre skew in the tax system is rooted in racism:

> White Alabamians have long resisted paying for the education of African American children. A popular belief has been that "everybody pays sales taxes"—white and black alike— while they assumed that black people did not own property. Thus some local districts, faced with a state mandate to raise

local property taxes for education or to raise the equivalent amount in sales taxes, have chosen to keep their property taxes very low and their sales taxes high.

And as if these inequities were not sufficiently disproportionate, Alabama is now phasing out the estate tax—another shift of the tax burden from the rich to the poor and middle class.

Helen Rivas believes that racism is also at the root of another of Alabama's social problems, the lack of an adequate public transportation system. As she points out,

> In 1961 the state adopted an amendment to the constitution to forbid the use of the gasoline tax to help pay for public transportation. All the money has to go for bridges and highways. That amendment was specifically inserted to keep black people from getting to white neighborhoods. Repealing that amendment is now one of the major things we're pushing for, but we're up against an unholy alliance of road builders, paving contractors, and some politicians.

## Fighting Predatory Lending

Rivas contends that racism is also behind a loophole in Alabama's law against predatory lending, a loophole that forces people who need a cash advance before payday to pay interest at rates of more than 1,000 percent.

It's called "payday lending." Suppose you run out of money to buy groceries or pay the rent and can't wait until payday. You write a personal check for the amount you want to borrow, add a fee for the lender, and leave the check as security. The fee can amount to $20 per $100 borrowed or 20 percent for a mere couple of weeks! On payday, you give the lender his $120, and get your check back. But if you still don't have the cash, the lender can hold the check for another two weeks and add an additional $20.

The victims, according to an Arise Policy Project fact sheet, are often elderly people who are fooled by the convenience and simplicity of payday loans. They overlook the fact that they are at least ten times more expensive than traditional small loans, which are capped by Alabama law at 36 percent: "The borrower must pay the principal and fees, pay a bank penalty—or risk prosecution on bad check charges," according to the fact sheet.

When pressure by Arise and its allies finally got the legislature to act, it drafted a law that redefined payday loans as "deferred presentment" of personal checks, thus neatly removing them from the limits of the small loans act and, while it set a ceiling, the maximum fee could still amount to three transactions at 17.5 percent each, or $70 for a sixty-day loan of $200. Although it was trumpeted as a reform, the legislation would in effect have made payday loans legal at just the moment they were being challenged in the courts. A middle-class family, meanwhile, can pay little more than $8 for a comparable cash advance on a credit card. These provisions were so onerous that Arise, which had been battling for years for real reform, persuaded its supporters in the legislature to help kill the bill. Real reform is still on the agenda.

Arise's priorities also include one-sided landlord-tenant regulations, as well as a death penalty moratorium that is literally a life-and-death issue for the disproportionately poor and black prisoners on death row.

If these issues form a long and challenging agenda, well, Arise did not get its name for nothing. A popular Alabama newspaper columnist commented that Arise and its Citizens' Policy Project are often on "the right but losing side." Arise activists acknowledge that it is often slow going and never easy, but they are not quitters. The professionals and volunteers who have dedicated themselves to this effort are confident that sooner or later they will be on the right *and winning* side. And they appreciate that their chances of prevailing are greatly boosted by the grants they receive from Veatch.

# People Organized in Defense of Earth and Its Resources
## *Resisting Environmental Racism*

A FAVORITE T-SHIRT of students at the University of Texas in Austin reads, "Keep Austin Weird." That sentiment reflects Austin's reputation as fairly liberal, at least compared to the rest of Texas. And, indeed, Austin can boast of such enlightened policies as encouraging smart growth, recycling, historic preservation, and protecting its drinking water. All are policies that any friend of the environment would welcome—unless you live east of Interstate 35.

That highway is Austin's great divide. To the west are the business and government centers, the university campus, and the more desirable neighborhoods. To the east, the community is primarily Mexican American, some of whom are recent immigrants, others third and fourth generation Texans whose forebears were here before the "Anglos." There are also smaller groups of African Americans and other minorities.

The outward appearance of East Austin is attractive, with many small two-bedroom houses that are currently being marketed as "cozy bungalows." But there are also empty lots, reminders of 1960s urban renewal, and the area is zoned for industry, so warehouses that store and use hazardous chemicals, auto repair shops, pawn shops, and liquor stores also abound. Worst of all, a power plant and a metal working shop stand directly across from a school. That jarring inconsistency accounts for the existence of People Organized in Defense of Earth and Its Resources (PODER) as well as its agenda.

Appropriately, PODER is located in the midst of this varied neighborhood in a small converted private house on Garden Street. Its office walls speak eloquently about its mission. One poster shows a woman in Native American dress standing on a rock, and the caption reads, "Only after the last tree has been cut down . . . only after the last river has been poisoned . . . only after the last fish has been caught—only then will you learn that money cannot be eaten." Surrounding it are clippings about PODER achievements, photos of demonstrations, awards presented by Raza and the Sierra Club, and to sum it all up a couple of bumper stickers: *You dump it, you drink it* and *It's Our Environment, Too.*

Dr. Sylvia Herrera, who has a master's degree in social work and a doctorate in health education, is PODER's health coordinator. Wearing Mexican-styled clothing, she gives visible proof of pride in her heritage. The director is Susana Almanza, who also wears Mexican patterns and, like Herrera, is a woman of color. Two of PODER's cofounders, they both trace their activism to childhood experiences. A teacher taped Herrera's mouth shut for speaking Spanish when she was seven, while Almanza learned "how you were treated if you were poor and speaking Spanish" when, at the age of five, she translated for her parents.

## PODER Means Power

Almanza explains why she and Herrera felt it was necessary to organize PODER:

> There is no other organization in all of Austin like ours. There are all the mainstream environmental groups like Environmental Defense Fund and Sierra Club, but no one

was really looking at how the environment interlocks with humanity. Yes, we must take care of the water, but we must also take care of the people who're drinking it. Yes, it was important to start recycling, but nobody bothered to ask where the recycled material should go, just as nobody bothered to wonder why one small community should take on the burden of a generating plant that benefits the whole city. You can't just look at the environment without looking at the human beings who are being impacted.

We're also unique in another way. In our community we have housing advocates and educational advocates, and so on, but only PODER looks at all the environmental justice issues that affect communities of color.

Herrera recalls the crystallizing 1991 event that led her to devote her energies to this cause. It was a newspaper notice that announced that Mobil Oil had filed a request to add an above-ground storage tank to an existing fifty-two-acre tank farm. "I happened to live only a couple of blocks away, so naturally that caught my attention," she notes. She called Almanza, who replied: "Sylvia, what are you doing reading public notices just before Christmas? Can't we take a break for the holidays?" No, they could not—the holidays have to wait, Herrera explained. The deadline for public comment was January 15.

Up to then, PODER's major concern had been a municipal effort to attract high-tech companies through tax breaks—companies that would provide jobs for residents of West Austin, but whose polluting facilities were to be built in East Austin where children, with some of the lowest educational attainment levels in the city, were least likely to qualify for future employment.

Now PODER, joined by a coalition of African American neighborhood groups, wrote letters to the Texas Air Control Board. They pointed out that the tank farm was located in a predominantly residential neighborhood; that several elementary schools were nearby; that expansion would further increase the emission of benzine and xylene, two known carcinogens, and that everyone in the neighborhood could smell the fumes. They not only wrote letters, but as Herrera recalls,

> We went door-to-door to find out about people's health problems. We developed a one-page survey and checked off whose children had nose bleeds, who had asthma, who had a lot of migraine headaches. A lot of them said, yes, we have this or that respiratory or other health problem, but they'd always thought that it just concerned their family. But as we shared the information, they began to realize that the whole neighborhood was having similar problems and that it had something to do with air violations at the tank farm.
>
> Then we held community meetings and organized a "toxic tour" for elected and school officials and the media. That got public attention and set off a series of investigations by different regulatory agencies.

That in itself represented a victory because the various city boards and commissions which should have done something about these problems had never taken any action, a consequence of what Herrera calls a political "ripple effect." Austin, she points out, is the largest US city that still elects its governing council at large, which effectively denies East Austin adequate representation. The council, in turn, appoints the members of boards and commissions. Until very recently the council never had a "green"—that is, environmentally sensitive—majority. Thus the tank farm polluted the air with impunity—until PODER got active. As Herrara explains,

> We organized a Tank Farm Citizens Monitoring Committee, made up of representatives of EAST as well as PODER. Then we held community meetings, and we kept after the regulatory agencies and elected officials—and in just eighteen months we were able to get them to relocate the tank farm. That was an outstanding achievement and in 2003 we celebrated the tenth anniversary of our victory.

That campaign has become the model for how we do our work. We set our own agenda, and then plan the strategy for achieving it. It is, for example, the model we're now applying in our battle to shut down the Holly Power Plant.

The Holly Power Plant is a municipal facility that is also stuck in the middle of East Austin. As Almanza and Herrera complained in a joint letter to the U.S. Environmental Protection Agency, "The Holly Power Plant emits harmful particulates into the air from fuel oil and natural gas combustion . . . Census data indicate that 85 percent of residents living near the plant are Latinos."

In 1997, Herrera continues, they thought the problem was solved:

> We were able to get the city council to agree to shut down two of the generating units by 1998, and the rest by 2005. They did in fact shut down two units in the fall of '98, but in the spring of '99 the city council rescinded its resolution because of the need for more energy. We complained that they didn't have an air permit, and in the fall of 2000 they finally filed for a permit from the Texas Commission on Environmental Quality that would allow them to exceed pollution limits for an additional ten years. We requested a public hearing and, finally, in December of 2002 they scheduled one. We asked around the neighborhood whether people had received the air permit public hearing notice and everybody said, "What are you talking about?"
>
> So we went to the hearing and asked them who they'd sent the notice to. They said that they'd sent it to only about four people who had requested the hearing, but we had kept copies of all the letters the neighbors had sent and which we had delivered in person, so they finally agreed to schedule another air permit hearing in March of 2003.

Testifying before the commission, Almanza said, "The Holly plant has a bad compliance record and should not be allowed to continue to operate. The ten-year air permit should be denied and the plant closed immediately."

PODER also focused on a noise study commissioned by the city, which documented that the noise exceeded acceptable levels for a residential area, as set by the Department of Housing and Urban Development. Through its own health questionnaire, PODER concluded that children in the elementary school two blocks away had difficulty concentrating and sleeping. The city responded with a noise abatement program, installing new windows in nearby homes. "The problem is that these are poor people," Herrera points out. "They can't afford central air conditioning, so now they had new windows but they had to keep them open."

Despite all these bureaucratic delays and broken promises, PODER has far from given up, and shutting down the generating plant is still high on its agenda.

## The Consequences of Gentrification

While the tank farm victory won PODER its Sierra Club Special Service Award, another issue has split the environmental coalition. That issue is gentrification. Sierra and other conservation groups are actively backing the city's current "smart growth" policy. To counteract urban sprawl and especially to protect the city's watershed west of Austin, the municipal government has encouraged people to move back to the center city. The catch, says Herrera, is that the smart growth relocation map ignores the fact that there are people already living in the area designated for redevelopment. That, in her mind, makes it a plan for removing the undesirable industries in East Austin—and for removing the African American and Mexican communities along with them: "They were designating East Austin as a desirable development zone, as if there were no people living here! They even started calling our area Central Austin, making the point that it's only five minutes away from downtown."

What followed matched the classic pattern of gentrification. Property values went up—then reassessment based on the first few sales raised taxes—so that people fell behind in their tax payments and then lost their property for failure to pay taxes. "Next people came in to buy the foreclosed properties at auction, made minor cosmetic changes, and flipped the property, tripling the price," Herrera explains. That, based on recent sales, further raised the neighbors' taxes. She continues,

> We've started holding workshops on how to protest your taxes, and to explain to people what's happening, because the official notices that are sent out are not in Spanish. We told people to take pictures of their houses, to get estimates of what it would cost to fix them up, to check on plumbing and electricity and the state of the foundation—all the things you need to prove that the house is not worth what the new assessment claims.

Then PODER found that the new people moving in were applying to have their homes qualify under historic zoning, thus entitling them to tax exemptions. So now the original residents got hit by a further tax hike because they were living next to historic homes. "We've been studying the census maps," Herrera says, "and they show that the African American and Mexican community is being moved ever further east."

As a former member of the Austin Planning Commission, Almanza has a good understanding of how what she calls "poor or racist land use policies" subject communities of color to environmental injustice.

> It's a battle that people of color, time and again, have lost: to urban renewal, to crime waves, to gentrification, and to the development or abandonment of property. This battle is not usually seen as an environmental issue, but in fact it is one of the most crucial of all urban environmental issues.

Even white flight, in addition to eroding the municipal tax base, is an environmental issue as "suburban commuters drive to the inner city for their livelihood during the day, only to leave their pollution behind at night."

During her term on the commission, Almanza worked with neighborhood leaders and the city council to change the zoning of numerous homes from industrial or commercial to residential. When the "green" city council got elected, it established neighborhood planning districts. Participating in this new planning process, PODER succeeded in having more than 600 properties rezoned—a huge victory for area residents.

But new problems keep coming up, and PODER, with the help of its Veatch grant, keeps working hard to solve them. The latest is that Austin, as part of its smart growth program, is encouraging mixed-income housing but, PODER asks, why are these units all slated for East Austin? "There's vacant land in other areas of the city," Herrera says. "Let's also build mixed-income communities in other neighborhoods."

## The Big Picture

Herrera summed up by stressing again how everything is connected—protection of the aquifer, smart growth planning, better public transportation, protection of historic homes—and the lives of people in East Austin:

> It's why we do environmental, economic, and educational studies. We're all for protecting the watershed and for smart growth and for recycling—they're all good things. All we want to know is how these things will impact the community we're living in. Take recycling. It's great. It's essential. But they put the recycling facility in our residential area, so we had heavy trucks going through our neighborhood with our kids walking to school alongside eighteen-wheelers, plus the noise of crushing glass in the middle of the night. We were finally able to get the city to buy out that facility, but it should never have been put there.

There is also a positive side to the interconnectedness of these issues, the opportunity to form alliances. It starts with enlisting the people in the affected neighborhoods, giving voice to those being victimized, and helping them to help themselves through leadership development. A measure of PODER's success is its organizational structure, which is headed by a board made up of representatives from different neighborhoods. These leaders attend both the PODER meetings and their neighborhood group board meetings, and they testify before the planning commission, the city council, and various state agencies. A parallel effort has succeeded in enlisting parents in the fight for better and safer schools. A weekly radio show helps to keep people informed and focused.

The next level of networking is to form alliances with other organizations with overlapping goals. A scientist associated with the state Sierra Club helped set up the air modeling program; technical and legal advice from the Texas Center for Policy contributed to the struggle to shut down the tank farm; support also came from Earth First and the Audubon Society. The only problem, Herrera says,

> Was they immediately wanted to position themselves as taking the lead. We said, we do want your support, but we don't want you to lead. That's not what we're about. We, the grassroots people, speak for ourselves. It took a little time, and we had to say, No, you're not the leader here: the community is, but eventually they accepted that.

> It happened again with the Holly issue. Someone in one of the environmental groups who had moved into the neighborhood decided she was going to lead this issue. We said, you have to respect the community leaders who are here and have been here for generations. We've been working on this for a long time. The same way in reverse on the watershed issue, we respect the fact that this was the primary issue for another organization, so we said to them, tell us how we can help.

A photograph in a recent issue of the PODER newsletter illustrates the triumphs that alliances can achieve. It was taken at the celebration of the tenth anniversary of the removal of the storage tanks and shows a smiling Dr. Herrera with Ken Oden, the former county attorney. It was Oden's civil and criminal investigation of the tank farm, responding to PODER's initiative, that persuaded the oil companies to relocate. It is very likely that neither could have done it alone. Certainly it would never have happened except for the initiative of two concerned women who decided it was time to start a community organization; who reached out first to their neighbors, then to city and state officials, then to allies, and then to the media. No ally has been more staunch and consistent in its support than the Veatch Program with its grants.

Steven Rossiter, an urban planner for the city, is quoted in *Sierra* magazine as admitting that the two women can be confrontational; that the city council is not always pleased to see them walking through its doors. But he acknowledges that "sometimes you're just not heard unless you get up in someone's face . . . [and] Susana and Sylvia have been effective in giving voice to issues that otherwise would not have gotten a hearing."

What motivates them, as Herrera puts it, is the proposition that "the environment is not only about birds and salamanders; it is also about people," while Almanza, who draws inspiration from her ethnic background, affirms that "there was a time when we were all sisters and brothers, the night sky our ceiling, the earth our mother, the sun our father, and our parents the leaders, and justice their guide."

Presumably you don't have to be poor or a member of a minority to be inspired by that ideal.

# SouthWest Organizing Project
## *Standing Up for Environmental Justice*

THE TERM "BUCKET BRIGADE" calls to mind a cooperative community effort to put out a fire.

The Bucket Brigade of the SouthWest Organizing Project (SWOP) is aptly named but the disaster it is fighting is incendiary only in the metaphorical sense. What SWOP is fighting is an Intel plant in Rio Ranches, New Mexico.

The company, in contrast to its slogan of "Intel Inside" does not keep all its pollutants inside. Instead, it spreads them into neighboring communities. So the SouthWest Organizing Project recruited volunteers to collect air samples in special plastic bags that are then sent to a laboratory for analysis, documenting the residents' complaints. Hence, the aptly named "bucket brigade."

Supplementing this effort, SWOP has bought an infrared spectrometry device that uses a laser to provide "real-time" readings and analyses of some ten thousand airborne chemical compounds. Reflecting SWOP's ability to form potent alliances—a characteristic of just about all Veatch grant recipients—the money to buy the device was raised from local donations by Corrales Residents for Clean Air and Water (CRCAW), and the operation is being conducted by teams of volunteers under the direction of retired scientists from New Mexico's Los Alamos National Laboratories. Rounding out the chain of cooperation, the monitor, which is mobile, is now in the home of a local resident. This effort, says CRCAW president Fred Marsh, himself a retired scientist, will settle once and for all the debate as to whether Intel's chip manufacturing plant is emitting toxins that cause headaches and nausea (let alone nasty odors). Meanwhile, the bucket brigade continues, because volunteers can catch some compounds that the laser monitor doesn't, and vice versa. None of this citizen action would be necessary, of course, if the state Environment Department had responded to SWOP's plea for intervention.

## Thinking Globally

Air pollution isn't the only environmental problem the Intel plant has caused, making it, for all the jobs it provides, a problematic neighbor. New Mexico is a dry state—dry in the literal sense. Not only is the area geologically a high desert, but for the last seven years it has suffered from a severe drought. Its aquifers are, therefore, a critical resource. But, as Michael Guerrero, SWOP's codirector, explains,

> Intel uses about four million gallons [of water] a day, and they get it right out of the aquifer. We fought their getting those water rights, but in 1997 the state engineers gave them nine years to keep pumping. But we haven't given up. We found out that Los Alamos National Laboratory has developed a process that uses up to 90 percent less water and produces far less hazardous chemicals. It's a closed-loop system using a carbon dioxide process, and as we understand it, IBM has already started using it. But despite the fact that Intel is an industry leader, with about an 80 percent market share, it insists that it needs to wait until there's more experience with the process.

SWOP took Intel to court but lost, so now it is trying to organize a shareholders' campaign. Concern about Intel's water use has also led SWOP to coordinate its efforts with an environmental group in Costa Rica, where the company built a plant right on top of a sensitive aquifer that had been designated by the municipality as an ecological zone barred to industry. They were, however, overruled by the national government.

This is another example of how globalization has forced U.S. grassroots organizations to look beyond our borders to solve home problems. To quote the organization's newsletter, "SWOP recognizes that our struggle for justice and peace is integrally linked with the liberation struggles of people throughout the world."

SWOP is also one of about fifty organizations that are cooperating in the Southwest Network for Environmental and Economic Justice (another Veatch grantee), which straddles the U.S./Mexican border. Launched in 1990 by some eighty activists, the network now has affiliates in four northern Mexican states, as well as Arizona, California, Texas, and New Mexico. According to former Veatch program officer Anannya Bhattacharjee, it is one of the most important networks in the environmental justice movement.

SWOP has also reached out to communities in Ireland, Israel, and Asia, seeking allies around the world to coordinate efforts to make Intel accountable to its "host" communities, and it sent a delegation, including youth delegates, to the Third World Social Forum in Porto Alegre, Brazil, in 2002.

Closer to home, SWOP, which serves the Chicano population in New Mexico primarily, has worked closely with the SAGE Council (Sacred Alliance for Grassroot Equality) which concentrates on Native American causes, such as the protection of petroglyphs threatened by development.

## Watering the Roots

To cultivate its grassroots base, SWOP sponsors a weekly get-together called *tardeada*, a Spanish word that Guerrero translates as "gathering":

> Every Friday afternoon we invite people to come over after work and join us on our patio. [The SWOP headquarters is

in a converted multi-story private house in a primarily blue-collar residential neighborhood, highly reminiscent of the Northwest Bronx Coalition offices.] Sometimes somebody talks about a certain topic, but mostly we just do a barbecue and it's more of a social activity. It's part of our effort to develop a deeper relationship with a broader group of people. We average about twenty-five people each time, and it's a way for [us] to get to know personally people [we] see at rallies or other activities where [we] don't really get a chance to know them. People really like it and it's important because it builds more of a team spirit.

The *tardeada* reflects a philosophy of community organizing that is a little different from that of most other grassroots organizations, in that it does not concentrate on membership growth. Instead SWOP pursues a "Fifty-seven Hundred Plan." As Guerrero explains,

Over the course of our almost twenty-five years of work we have built a database of some fifty-seven hundred people in the state of New Mexico who have participated in one or another of our activities. Instead of doing outreach to add more names to the list, we decided to focus on the folks already on our list, with special attention on the three thousand or so who live in the Albuquerque area. This year [2003] we have a city council election in four districts, so we broke the list down even further to identify the eleven hundred who live in those districts. Through door-to-door visits, we are trying to make sure that they are registered to vote, and that they get our series of education leaflets on the issues in the election, especially the three issues of outstanding importance: public safety, economic development, and the city budget. We also hold workshops on these issues.

In other words, we're trying to create more literacy about decision-making in our city. We want people to understand that public safety doesn't mean more cops but economic justice and community centers for our youth. Our goal is to have some five hundred people become actively engaged in the decision-making in the city. We realize that we can't accomplish that in just one year, and while we have been turning out people at budget hearings, the educational process has to be long term.

Not surprisingly, this kind of grassroots organizing has not made SWOP popular with Albuquerque's pro-growth mayor, who used the reaction to the 9/11 tragedy as an opportunity to brand SWOP as "terrorist."

For at least the last twenty years, the politics of Albuquerque have been dominated by developers, with the mayor as their unfailing ally. Herrero describes a bitter battle between developers and grassroots community groups. The monetary resources, of course, are seriously mismatched, and the mayor is fighting SWOP in every way he can:

- He claimed that SWOP wanted to shut down not only Intel but all local industry.

- When SWOP questioned the bombing of Afghanistan, he denounced it as pro-Taliban.

- He vetoed a city council bill to review the tax breaks given to corporations, citing as his reason SWOP's support of the bill.

- Finally, adding injury to insult, the mayor authorized taking $1.9 million from the Family and Community Services budget to fund the police "Gang Unit."

That last item is not the first time the mayor opposed youth programs. In place of requests for greater investments in community centers and youth activities, he called for increased funding for police and additional jails, saying, "I need another officer on the street damn it, not another community center."

According to Mike Guerrero, "We did a study of the condition of the community centers, and found out that they were dismal. Some of the directors are actually using their own money to provide programs, and they are having to turn some kids away because there simply isn't enough money to provide services for all age groups." Victoria Rodriguez, a SWOP organizer, adds, "According to our research, one police officer's overtime pay was more than two community centers' annual budgets combined." Unfortunately, six of the nine members of the city council back the mayor's priorities and only two of the seven school board members support progressive policies. Despite the imbalance, SWOP was at least able to defeat a plan to arm security guards during school hours.

In response to the city's neglect, SWOP has been training youth to work on their own problems. Recently it completed a youth rights curriculum that is used to teach high school students basic organizing skills. And to promote cultural activities, SWOP funds Jovenes Unidos, which sponsors theater, music, and arts programs.

## Tackling Problems Community by Community

According to federal guidelines, a *colonia* is a squatter community within a hundred miles of the Mexican border, such as those in Texas described in the chapter "Valley Interfaith." These criteria mean that because of their location, the people in Parajito Mesa were not eligible for federal funding—but they qualified in every other way. Located in an unincorporated area of Bernalillo County in the outskirts of Albuquerque, they lacked safe drinking water, sewage, electricity, or even paved roads until, as Guerrero describes, SWOP went to bat for them:

> We haven't been able to solve all their problems, but we're getting close. First we raised enough money through individual donations to enable them to buy a road grader, so they were able to at least grade their own roads.
>
> Then we helped them organize a mutual water users' association and to get it recognized by the state as a legally constituted authority, in other words as a quasi-governmental agency. That means it can assess fees and pay engineers to design a safe drinking water system. Because the mesa is too

spread out to make it economically feasible to lay water lines, a truck will deliver the water to the homeowners. Everyone will get a 500-gallon tank and a solar generator to run a pump as well as provide some lighting for the house.

Finally, each house will get a septic tank, and while there are still some legal issues to be resolved, primarily so that government vehicles can go up there to help them, we've had promises of funding from both state and federal agencies.

That's a lot to accomplish for a staff of only eight full-time people.

Another community organizing effort concerns waste contamination in a place called Wells Park where a company collects medical waste from hospitals all over New Mexico and from nearby El Paso, Texas. There used to be an incinerator, but a community organization called Concerned Citizens of Southern Park succeeded, with the help of SWOP, in getting it shut down, substituting a transfer station. Now, however, the company wants to convert it again, establishing a sterilization facility. They assure the neighbors that it is a safer, cleaner process, but even if so, it still stands smack in the middle of a residential area.

In typical bureaucratic fashion the state had already approved the application before the residents knew it had been filed. When residents tried to negotiate some conditions, such as monetary compensation for neighborhood improvements, they were told that it was too late: The process was already too far along.

The list of problems goes on. In South Valley the issue is serious hazardous waste contamination from a private landfill that's trying to expand, while in Veguita, a rural community about an hour south of Albuquerque, contaminated drinking water threatens the residents' health. The interesting part is that in this instance it was a state agency, the New Mexico Environment Department, that turned to SWOP for help after determining that one in four wells tested had high nitrate levels, some twenty times above safe standards. In response, SWOP organizers went door-to-door to let the residents know about free water testing sponsored by the department and formed a core group of community leaders to develop both short- and long-term plans for a safe water source.

No matter how generous the support of local contributors, plus grants from the Veatch Program and other progressive funders, an organization like SWOP can never compete with the monies its opponents collect from developers, polluters, and entrenched politicians. Instead, SWOP's long-term success depends on people power: the ability to organize those it is trying to help.

In June 2003, SWOP held its first statewide assembly, bringing together the leaders of previously isolated community efforts in South Valley, Veguita, Parajito Mesa, and Albuquerque itself. Looking to the future, it maintains a highly successful summer youth internship program.

Young leaders, mostly teenagers, have an opportunity to work on a daily basis with SWOP staff on such critical programs as voter registration, *colonia* improvement, and monitoring Intel. Two former youth interns are now full-time staff organizers, and others are active members of the youth leadership group. Indeed, Michael Guerrero was the first intern. He went on to enroll in a fellowship program that SWOP was running at the time and join the staff as a field organizer, and he became codirector in 1987. He has had ample opportunity, therefore, to assess the importance of Veatch funding. Like his colleagues in similar organizations, Guerrero stresses how important it is that the Veatch grant is awarded as general support. Out of SWOP's budget of slightly over half a million, the Veatch grant constitutes only about 5 percent, but because it is not designated for a specific purpose SWOP can use it to fund critical areas and unexpected needs. "It's absolutely the best way to support an organization like ours," he says.

As someone who has been active in community organizing since the Reagan administration, Guerrero assesses the trends in the ongoing fight for social justice:

> Sometimes it seems like one series of setbacks after another. Certainly it's been an uphill battle for decades, and now we have all the scary stuff that Bush is doing.
>
> Something in me, though, makes me feel hopeful. That hope comes from seeing what people are doing for themselves; it comes from knowing that organizing works; it comes from the largely successful work we've been able to do for some twenty-five years. And the hope comes from building direct relationships with people, having real conversations, and finding out again and again that there is a lot more common ground than we realize.
>
> Regardless of all the stuff we sometimes go through, just imagine if SWOP were not here! When things get really bad, when they don't know where else to go, people call us. It shows the importance of grassroots community organizing. Also, I think we're getting more sophisticated, more skilled in how we go about organizing. And finally, I see these things happening not only here but all around the country.
>
> The greatest weakness is that we don't have a national infrastructure. Joining with like-minded organizations in the Southwest Network is a first step. It means that we have a regional effort and that there's a vehicle for us to get to know like-minded people. And we've hooked up with a process called Grassroots Global Justice, which grew out of the delegations that met at the World Social Forum and, which, incidentally, Veatch is also supporting. So, finally, what makes me hopeful is that there is so much activity going on around the world, a huge global dialogue. We in the United States have to be part of that dialogue; to become less insulated. We need to make that connection.

Perhaps it is his own background that gives Guerrero such a broad perspective. Not only does he work every day with Chicanos, Anglos, and Pueblo Indians, he himself (as a Pacific Islander) is a member of yet another ethnic group. He started his career as a fighter for social justice by helping the Chamoru people of Guam resist colonization, and pressuring the U.S. military to clean up its waste sites. But probably the greatest asset he brings to solving the grinding problems he tackles every day is his indomitable sense of hope and his ability to discuss them dispassionately, even with a smile. As he says, "Just being able to survive and have an impact is tremendously important."

# The Indigenous Environmental Network
## *Protecting the First People from Exploitation*

LIKE PODER AND SWOP, the Indigenous Environmental Network (IEN) is a self-help, grassroots organization dedicated to fighting environmental injustice inflicted on an embattled minority. But while the situation of Native Americans is in many ways similar to those of other ethnic groups, it is also in some ways unique. In 2002, Tom Goldtooth, IEN's executive director, visited the Unitarian Universalist Congregation at Shelter Rock on Long Island as guest speaker. While thanking the congregation for the help it was giving IEN through Veatch, he also made it clear that the battle against environmental racism is far from won. As he explains,

> Even as we stand as brothers and sisters with African Americans, Mexicans, and Asian people, we have differences that are based on our legal and political relationships with the government. In return for the land we gave to the United States, we negotiated treaties under which we reserved rights, and those rights are secured within what is called a trust responsibility between the government and our tribes

and our land. Part of that trust responsibility requires the protection of our lands and our water and the health of our people.

But instead of protection, what the federal government all too often permitted or inflicted was exploitation. In the early 1990s, Goldtooth, then director of the environmental program for the Ojibwa tribe in Minnesota—together with other tribal leaders— began to examine the prevailing pattern of environmental injustice in Indian* country. In 1991, at the spiritual site of Bear Butte in South Dakota, native environmental activists met to devise a common course of action, and from this gathering, according to Goldtooth, the idea of IEN was born:

> We started to look at such issues as thousands of unmanaged open dumps in Indian countries, because tribes were vulnerable to private waste industries that came to them with proposals for working partnerships that allowed them to build large municipal landfills, toxic landfills, and incinerators. In addition, we found that EPA [the U.S. Environmental Protection Agency] had neglected its fiduciary responsibility, and tribal environmental protection programs were not provided financial resources comparable to what was being paid to state governments.

IEN tackled these problems on two fronts—by raising policy issues with governmental agencies such as the Environmental Protection Agency and the Bureau of Indian Affairs, which for decades had failed to collect the royalties due to the tribes, and by educating tribal leaders so that the government would find it harder to take advantage of them in the future. Goldtooth continues,

> Few tribes had any kind of environmental protection provisions. Even fewer had environmental specialists. The things that most U.S. citizens take for granted—that their state, county, or

---

* Goldtooth and other tribal activists use such terms as "Indian" and "Indian country" without hesitation, even if it is not considered politically correct by some outsiders.

city is watching what's being done to the environment—was not happening on Indian lands. Without a staff person keeping an eye on things, tribal leadership often did not have adequate information. They were told that the dumping was safe, that they need not worry about what was being dumped, and the company's contractors were doing the environmental assessment.

IEN emerged out of this reality. We are a network of grassroots tribal members who began to stand up in the early '90s, telling tribal governments—as well as the federal government—we don't want these private waste industries in our backyard. But until IEN came along, there was no national entity to provide these grassroots protesters with technical support or to act as a national voice.

## Going to the Hot Spots

By 1995, IEN was sufficiently well established to be able to hire staff, and having previously served as volunteer board coordinator and national spokesperson, Goldtooth took over as national director. Now the network has a staff of nine, three of whom work at critical locations reflecting the network's current emphases, mining, oil, and toxic chemicals. Goldtooth points out,

> Over the years, we have worked with over 200 indigenous communities and organizations and that is very significant, very important. But now we want to focus on a limited number of issues, and one of those issues is mining. We asked all of our two hundred communities: Are you affected by mining? Then we told our mining organizer to work with those that are. The same with oil and toxic chemicals.

Sayo:kla Kindness, stationed in the Oneida reservation in Wisconsin, is organizer of the Indigenous Mining Campaign, working with communities affected by mines, whether of uranium, coal, hard rock, or metals. Some of these communities are well organized; others are almost wholly dependent on the technical and organizing support provided by IEN.

Shawna Larson tackles toxins. An Athabascan Alaska native, she works in partnership with Alaskan Communities Against Persistent Organic Pollutants (POPS), which pays half her salary. She seeks to educate grassroots people and their leaders about the dangers of toxic chemicals spewed out by mines, oil refineries, plastics factories, even agriculture. Nor is local contamination the only problem. As Goldtooth explains, many toxic chemicals whose use is banned in the United States can still be manufactured for export, but often they are highly volatile and escape into the atmosphere. "Somehow through this process they migrate to colder climates," he says. "Thus there are high levels of these chemicals in the food systems in places like Alaska, and since Alaska natives depend on traditional [hence local] food supplies, they are particularly vulnerable."

This phenomenon is more than a health threat. It also undermines the indigenous culture, Goldtooth maintains: "Not only in Alaska but in Canada, and especially along the coastline, many of our Indian people have a very close relationship with our traditional food systems—the livestock culture, the buffalo culture, the prairie land. Once these food systems are contaminated and our people stop eating them, we stand to lose our culture and then our language."

The third IEN priority is addressed by a program it calls "Red Oil." Alaska, with its oil and gas resources and the threat of oil exploration in the Arctic National Wildlife Refuge, is at special risk. Clayton Thomas-Muller, the designated organizer, is based in Vancouver, British Columbia, and works in partnership with Project Underground, a nonnative environmental organization headquartered in Berkeley, California.

Thomas-Muller is a circuit rider, visiting indigenous communities, finding out what their needs are and what has worked and not worked in fighting oil and gas development, and providing needed training. He also brings communities together to collaborate on the state, provincial, and regional levels. In late 2003, IEN held an organizing meeting of six tribes in Oklahoma that are affected by oil exploration or production. Similar meetings are scheduled for Montana and Canada.

The partnership with Project Underground has worked well; in fact Thomas-Muller received his training at its headquarters. "We are also working with Sierra Club in Flagstaff, Arizona, on water and mining issues," Goldtooth says, citing another successful alliance. But alliances with mainstream environmental organizations do not always work out smoothly. Like PODER, IEN has found that "there's a lot of arrogance within some of them. We and our constituents are very much concerned that we speak for ourselves, and many of our communities are very vulnerable. So when a predominantly white organization comes in and tries to give all the answers, instead of allowing them to develop their own programs and make their own decisions, it can be very frustrating."

One of the sources of tension is that environmental issues in Indian communities tend to be closely tied to issues of poverty, lack of employment, and poor housing, and single-focus environmental organizations may not wish to get involved in these more controversial problems. Hence, Goldtooth says,

> Our role has had to be to be a voice, to be an advocate for the empowerment of our communities, so our focus has to go beyond strictly environmental issues. Sometimes that has meant that we take positions that mainstream enviros find threatening. Also they don't take it too kindly when indigenous people at the same table with them display the same level of knowledge they have, and they find it hard to act appropriately.

## For All People

The criteria for ecological partnership, according to Goldtooth, must be based on four principles: the indigenous peoples' rights to the land and to self-determination; honesty, transparency, and good faith; prior and informed consent; and, finally, respect and recognition of their cultures, languages, and spiritual beliefs.

He delivered this message to the World Summit on Sustainable Development in Johannesburg in 2002 on behalf of more than three hundred indigenous peoples from all parts of the world who had gathered just before the World Summit for a conference of their own.

Goldtooth also said, "We reaffirm our relationship to Mother Earth and our responsibility to the youth and coming generations to uphold peace, equity, and justice." Then he warned that "ecosystems . . . continue to be degraded increasingly. We are in crisis. We are in an accelerating spiral of climate change that will not abide unsustainable greed." These concerns, of course, are not limited to indigenous peoples, as Goldtooth pointed out, so "we are holding the line not just for us; we are holding it for all people." Specifically regarding the needs of indigenous peoples, he stressed:

> We reaffirm our rights to self-determination; to own, control, and manage our ancestral land, seas, and territories, waters and other resources. It is important indigenous peoples be recognized as peoples, under international law. Our lands and territories are at the core of our existence—we are the land and the land is us—we are the water and the water is us. We have a distinct spiritual and material relationship with our lands and territories, and they are inextricable linked to our survival.

Goldtooth then pointed out that economic globalization constitutes one of the main obstacles to the recognition of the rights of indigenous peoples. Threats include not only mining and oil extraction, but dams that flood traditional lands, and trade policies that drive people off their land, creating homelessness, poverty, and disease. He also deplored tourism development that leads to exploitation of native lands and territories.

In light of the global aspect of such environmental problems, IEN is networking with indigenous peoples in Venezuela, Bolivia, and Africa, while at the same time building awareness of the local impact of globalization among its affiliates in the United States.

## Sustainable Communities

A theme that emerges powerfully from all statements on behalf of the Indigenous Environmental Network is the intricate connection between environmental/ecological issues and the need to build sustainable communities. Many of the communities IEN works with are in dire straits, Goldtooth says, and are therefore highly vulnerable to industries that make promises of economic gain if the tribe permits mining, oil drilling, or other unsustainable and contaminating practices.

In 1998, for example, two residents of the Rosebud Sioux Reservation, Oleta Menansky and Eva Iyotte, found out that the reservation's tribal council, with the backing of the Bureau of Indian Affairs, was negotiating a deal with Bell Farms, one of the nation's largest pork producers, to build a four-thousand-acre hog breeding facility, designed to raise 859,000 animals per year. According to a report in *National Wildlife*, that many pigs would have produced more feces and urine than the entire human population of South Dakota, would have used 1.6 million gallons of the reservation's scarce water per day, and would have required liquid manure lagoons totaling 550 acres.

Suing under the terms of the National Environmental Policy Act, a grassroots organization formed by the two women eventually won its case in the Supreme Court, only to be sued for damages by Bell Farms—an increasingly popular polluters' tactic.

## The Spiritual Dimension

In an interview with *In Motion* magazine, Goldtooth sums up the belief underlying IEN's work:

> Through our culture we are taught to have respect for our Earth, that we call our Mother. Our Earth is sacred, and we strive to maintain a harmonious relationship to the land in everything we do. Our farmers use seeds that have been handed down from generation to generation . . . and through

our traditional knowledge have been created to fit our environment and sustain us.

No wonder another plank in the IEN platform is resistance to the pressures from corporate farming interests and multinational chemical companies to use genetically modified seeds and industrialized farming practices. In addition to the economic and environmental issues that confront all farmers, Native Americans feel that biologically engineered seeds do not have a creative spirit. Thus, Goldtooth concludes that "the whole ideology of Western development imposed on our peoples" is in conflict with the basic belief in the "creative power of Mother Earth and Father Sky. It's called the creative principle."

## Battling the Bureau of Indian Affairs

As a network rather than a membership organization, IEN has formed alliances in its first ten years with more than 150 native community-based groups, tribal communities, and tribal environmental programs. This growth in networking has enabled it to interact with more than five thousand individuals—leaders, staff members, and volunteers, making it an information clearinghouse for American Indian and Alaskan native communities and providing them with both technical assistance and organizational help.

IEN also struggles with federal agencies on behalf of indigenous communities. In addition to fighting for fair funding allocations from the Environmental Protection Agency, IEN has also tackled the bureaucracy most intimately concerned with Native Americans: the Bureau of Indian Affairs (BIA).

In violation of its responsibility to protect Indian resources, BIA has often served as a Trojan Horse that takes advantage of naïve, incompetent, or, in some cases, even corrupt tribal governments, persuading them to negotiate leases and contracts that led to both environmental and financial depredation. In recent years for example, when IEN and others demanded to know what happened to monies collected by BIA on behalf of its "wards," it turned out that billions in mineral and grazing royalties had been diverted or mismanaged. As a result of IEN joining with other organizations to insist on accountability, they were able to achieve a tenfold increase in the amount of funding going to the rightful recipients. But this issue is far from settled.

IEN intervention has also strengthened tribal democracy, helping the younger generation to challenge entrenched tribal governments that were often prodevelopment and willing to sign one-sided contracts and leases. In helping those who want to change these policies, IEN, as it reports to the Veatch Program, "has become a mechanism that opens constructive dialogue between tribal members and their tribal governments."

While the process is slow and sometimes painful, IEN leaders have a long-term perspective that keeps them from becoming discouraged. "We have always operated from the principle of basing our decisions on how they will affect our next seven generations," says an IEN policy statement. Reflecting this long-term perspective, in 2001 IEN launched a youth program that offers leadership training and training for new trainers.

They will have their work cut out for them. The global oil and mining operations IEN is battling are as relentless as they are powerful. Tom Goldtooth observes that these interests "would prefer that we become assimilated and acculturated. But we still have our languages; we still have our culture. We have not mainstreamed. We haven't lost who we are. And we are making strides in obtaining recognition for our rights to our homeland."

And as Goldtooth also likes to point out, in holding the line on their own behalf, they are also holding it for other people, making IEN a natural ally of all who care about the environment.

Once a year, the Shelter Rock congregation celebrates Veatch Sunday. In 2003 the guest speaker was Ernie Cortés (third from left), southwest regional director of the Industrial Areas Foundation, shown here with that year's Veatch board of governors vice chair Jill Hyer, chair Rich Guilbert, and Veatch executive director Marjorie Fine.

Public Policy and Education Fund of New York recruits more than 1,300 community members to rally at New York's city hall in support of after-school programs.

Seniors organized by the Public Policy and Education Fund of New York demonstrate against high pharmaceutical prices and efforts to privatize Social Security.

The Chinese Staff and Workers' Association kicks off its campaign against sweatshops in the United States by launching a boycott against clothing manufacturer Liberty Apparel.

Chinese and Latino youth rally in support of PODER's Common Roots Program.

Seminary students affiliated with Interfaith Worker Justice march on the picket line to show solidarity with striking workers at the Congress Hotel in Chicago.

Once a year, members of the Unitarian Universalist Congregation at Shelter Rock and Veatch Program staff members visit grant recipients in the New York City area. This is the seventh such event, taking place in 2004. After a similar tour the year before, one member said, "I take great pride in the work of this congregation through the Veatch Program. Veatch grantmaking expresses my principles as a Unitarian Universalist."

The First Unitarian Church of San Jose received Veatch support to strengthen its social justice ministry. It is one of several UU congregations that receive such support.

After a five-year boycott supported by a number of UU congregations, the Farm Labor Organizing Committee was able to get the Mount Olive Pickle Company to sign a contract covering some eight thousand Mexican guest workers. The Farm Labor Research Project, a Veatch grantee, actively supported the effort to organize farm workers in North Carolina.

Members of the New Jersey Work Environment Council enjoy a moment of victory as Governor McGreevey signs an executive order instructing state agencies to be more responsive to issues of environmental justice.

Working with United Food and Commercial Workers Local 1500, Veatch grantee New York Jobs with Justice organized a series of media events to mobilize support for immigrant deli workers.

The United States Student Association and its Midwest Academy—both supported by Veatch grants—assemble after receiving training in community organizing.

Love Makes a Family held a Marriage Equality Rally in 2004 to show its support of equal rights for those subjected to social, economic, and legal discrimination due to sexual orientation or gender identity.

South Florida Jobs with Justice holds a Grassroots Organizing Weekend to teach leadership and organizing skills for emerging leaders in the struggle for workplace justice.

The SouthWest Organizing Project (SWOP) organized demonstrations against a local Intel plant to keep it from contaminating the environment, an example of environmental injustice.

In 2004, the Los Angeles City Council passed a landmark law that gives communities greater control over the siting of box retailers like Wal-Mart. The vote was the culmination of a two-year campaign led by Los Angeles Alliance for a New Economy.

Site visits are an important part of the Veatch Program's efforts to keep in touch with its grantees. On their 2004 annual tour, staff and board members traveled to Florida, including a visit with the Miami Workers Center, a grassroots membership organization of low-wage and no-wage workers who are fighting poverty and powerlessness.

As part of its mission to improve the working conditions of restaurant workers, the Restaurant Opportunities Center of New York is hoping to revolutionize the restaurant industry by launching employee-owned co-ops. Dedicated to food quality, service excellence, and employee welfare, these restaurants will also integrate the concepts of sustainable agriculture and support of local producers. The prototype will be launched in New York City in the fall of 2005.

David Fleischer, director of organizing and training for the National Gay and Lesbian Task Force, helps volunteers in Miami, Florida, defeat a ballot initiative aimed at repealing a section of a human rights ordinance intended to protect against discrimination based on sexual orientation. Waiting for his turn to speak is Wilson Cruz, a local activist.

# The Northwest Bronx
# Community and Clergy Coalition
## *Saving a Community from Destruction*

THE VISION OF the Veatch Program is rooted in Unitarian Universalist values, and none is given greater emphasis than promoting the democratic process. Thus Veatch uses its grants to support "what is right in America and loyally critiquing what is wrong." Few communities have had greater need of constructive citizen participation than New York City's northernmost borough, the Bronx.

The problems of the Bronx roused national attention when the headlines screamed "The Bronx Is Burning." Things are not as bad as they were in 1977, when Bill Moyers, then with the CBS network, alerted the nation to the epidemic of arson that was wrecking a once vibrant, affordable residential section of New York, while the late U.S. senator Daniel Patrick Moynihan compared the South Bronx to Berlin at the end of World War II. If things have improved, the Northwest Bronx Community and Clergy Coalition, a Veatch grantee, deserves much of the credit, but there are still enough problems to keep both its volunteers and its staff, headed by executive director Mary Dailey, extremely busy.

Like Andrea Cole and Kim Bobo, or for that matter Marjorie Fine, Dailey seems low-key and pleasantly relaxed at first. It's only

when listening to her that one realizes that she, too, has a backbone
of steel; that she is quietly but ferociously dedicated to tilting our
society toward justice and fairness. And like Cole and Bobo, she
realizes that for democracy to work, people have to feel that they
have some control over the way they live—to be able to earn a living wage—to live in decent housing—to send their children to
safe and effective schools.

Dalma De La Rosa, a leading coalition volunteer and a seasoned veteran in all these efforts, recollects,

> When I came from Puerto Rico, we lived in what was called
> Spanish Harlem. When I was about twelve, we moved to the
> Bronx. In those days, you moved to the Bronx because you
> were going up a notch, and we moved into a beautiful apart-
> ment building. Then the bad times came: the buildings were
> burning. Our neighbors in the back, the landlord burned the
> building. I had friends who used to come visit me, and they'd
> say, "You know what the perfume of the Bronx is? Smoke.
> When we get off the train, we immediately smell the smoke."
> They were hard years to go through. It was horrible.

As one apartment house after another was emptied of its residents, they were replaced by drug dealers and rats. It looked like
the end of an entire borough. That, De La Rosa says, is how she
became involved in the coalition in 1984:

> That was the year when the landlord of our building aban-
> doned it. It was in the middle of winter. We were cold and
> went into the basement and found there was no working
> boiler. Many of the apartments in the building had broken
> windows, broken walls, and we decided that we would all get
> together and try to see if we could fix the boiler.

> We did the best we could to get the boiler fixed, but we didn't
> realize what would happen when hot water hit the frozen
> pipes. Water was cascading down the front of the building,
> cascading from one apartment to another. The mailman used
> to ask, "Are people still living here?" One day an organizer

from the Coalition walked in and said: "You people need help. We're having a meeting with the Deputy Commissioner of Housing. Would you like to participate?"

I went to a planning meeting and met one of the organizers, a tall handsome man, by the name of Brian O'Toole, and I thought, this is great. This wonderful man is going to talk to them about my problems. I thought the organizers are going to do all the work. Then I found out the organizers don't do the talking. The leaders do the talking. The organizers just help you with information and point you in the right direction. Then you go and do it yourself. Believe me, I learned the hard way.

De La Rosa became a coalition leader and eventually its president. As she says self-deprecatingly, "From then on I haven't been able to shut my mouth." At first her concern was about housing, but she soon realized that the problem is much more complex than that:

There were drugs in our street, destroying our neighborhoods, and graffiti—whatever you fixed today, graffiti would destroy it tomorrow. So I joined every committee I could get my hands on. When crack came into our neighborhood, I became part of the Safe Streets Committee. We did a march on Fordham Road [a major shopping street] and the Grand Concourse [the once-elegant north-south thoroughfare]. We closed them both: two thousand people saying that not everyone in the Bronx uses drugs, that we're drug free and we want the police to work with us to make sure that drugs are taken off our streets. It was a great show of solidarity. It was great, fantastic.

Speaking of graffiti, it was Sistas and Brothas United (SBU), the coalition's youth organization, that realized cleaning them up was hopeless, that SBU was just making nice blank walls for "taggers" to come and scrawl their fancy signatures. "We prefer to have a mural than just people's signatures," says Laura Vázquez, a coalition youth organizer. "We identify the spots that attract graffiti and we talk to the residents and find out what kind of mural they'd like to see put up. Something that depicts the community in a positive way. Then we have the kids paint a mural. The taggers pretty much leave those alone." But first, there were more serious problems to solve.

## Neighbor Against Neighbor

The people of the Bronx were up against powerful enemies—some of them were their fellow residents. As Jill Jonnes writes in her book, *South Bronx Rising*, "In a frenzy of arson, greed and destruction, many willingly reaped the gains—landlords, tenants, junkies and finishers." *Finishers* were the ghouls sent in by landlords anxious to drive out the remaining tenants. They would rip out pipes and boilers—anything of value; set fires; and resort to violence if further "persuasion" was needed. "A citizenry annihilated its own city for profit," Jonnes reports. "This was not just another slum, but a city almost obliterated." The authorities meanwhile seemed helpless or indifferent.

As the blight spread rapidly from the south to the north and west, "South Bronx" became not a geographic term but shorthand for an accelerating pathology. Block by block, white flight drained the community of its economic core; rent delinquency and van-dalism persuaded more and more landlords to milk their proper-ties, stinting on maintenance and services and eventually walking away. In some cases, they burned their own buildings to collect insurance money. Welfare tenants, feeling trapped, set other fires so as to gain priority on waiting lists for municipal housing.

Once Bill Moyers focused the nation's attention on the Bronx, it became, Jonnes says, "a terrific stage for passing politicians." The Pope, presidents, and "radicals, journalists, assorted do-gooders, and hustlers of every hue" all got their moment on television, but the one thing they did not do was solve the problems.

That was left to local initiative, starting with Fordham University, a venerable Jesuit institution just on the edge of the encroaching civic destruction. Fordham appointed Paul Brant, a seminarian, to the new position of community liaison; in turn, he asked the Catholic pastors for support, though as Brant recalls, "They were all scared except for one." Brant also recruited two neighborhood organizers, one of whom had been trained in Saul Alinsky-style tactics. (Saul Alinsky is considered the father of modern American grassroots radicalism.) Jonnes quotes Brant as saying, "We were up against a stagnant bureaucracy and a real estate and banking complex which had written off that part of the Bronx." Meanwhile insurance companies refused to provide coverage for Bronx buildings. Even the city's community development funds did not get to the Bronx; the common attitude was: "Forget it. The arsonists will be there any day now."

Brant decided to meet the challenge by forming an ecumenical nonprofit coalition covering eight Catholic parishes. With $15,000 from a local savings bank and $40,000 the parishioners put in their collection plates, the organization was able to hire six full-time organizers to back up the volunteers with advice and training. It was just about this time, in the mid-1980s, that Mary Dailey joined the staff as a neighborhood organizer. "Together community leaders and staff can move mountains that neither could move alone," she says, and volunteer leader Karen Washington bears this out, saying: "When people come to the coalition to ask for help, they are told, 'Go back and form a homeowners' association.'" Staff organizers show them how, and under the slogan "Don't Move! Improve!" neighbors set up not-for-profit housing corporations, rescued threatened buildings, and even rebuilt some that had been abandoned.

## Fighting Back

That was one prong of the strategy. The other—tremendously helped by the local bishop—was to lean on savings banks and insurance companies to reverse their "redlining" policies. (Redlining is the practice of refusing to give loans to certain neighborhoods that are considered high-risk.) It took years of negotiation, picketing and demonstrations, meetings with politicians, and badgering of city agencies, but finally the coalition was able to persuade Aetna Insurance to share the risk of writing policies. Once brokers realized that there was money to be made, they began to offer coverage. But perhaps "persuade" is not quite the right word. Persuasion involved filling ten school buses to go to Washington as part of a National People's Action protest at the National Association of Insurance Companies, and taking over the building. At last, some community development funds made their way to the Bronx, paying for such capital improvements as sewer construction, subway station repair, and park renovation. In 1980, after six years of coalition efforts, only one building was lost.

Mary McLoughlin's experience demonstrates the extent of the turnaround. When her landlord tried to drive out the tenants by stopping garbage collection and hiring a nasty building superintendent, "Many people moved because the place was dirty and they weren't into being insulted." Then, in a well-established tactic, the landlord removed the furnace. But some tenants fought back, even when a retaining wall collapsed. They took the landlord to court, stuck with the case for two years, attended more than a hundred court hearings and meetings with city agencies—and finally won their case. "The coalition helped us right down the line," says McLoughlin. "They gave technical assistance and drove us to court and provided backup. I said to myself, 'This is a good building. I am not going to move. I am not going to allow a lousy landlord to deprive me of a place to live.'"

Slowly things began to look up. One priest who had been moved from the South Bronx described the change vividly. Father John Jenik told Jonnes, the source of much of this history,

> I had tried to organize [the previous parish] . . . but one after another the buildings just disappeared. When those buildings went, the guts just spilled out; the mattresses were half out the front doors, as if the buildings were regurgitating their insides. Then the supermarket burned down and it was a problem for people to even shop for food. We were all amazed how fires just ripped through and nothing was done.
>
> When I came to Our Lady of Refuge I looked around and said, "It's going to happen here." I saw it creeping across

Fordham Road [which the coalition considered its "Maginot Line"]. But the coalition was very savvy and they had expertise and altruism. When buildings were abandoned in the South Bronx no one protested. When buildings went here, we said we have to do something, and we did.

## A Growing Track Record

A bouncy, dynamic woman who laughs easily as she recalls the trials and triumphs she has witnessed, by 2003 Mary Dailey headed an organization of some forty-five hundred members, with more than two hundred fifty active leaders. Like those of most community organizations, the coalition's headquarters are far from posh. In fact, cluttered or even shabby might be more apt descriptions, with files stacked on every available chair, and the hats and jackets of visiting volunteers piled in the corners—signs that whatever funds are available, such as those provided by Veatch grants, are spent on programs, not show.

Recruiting volunteers is a continuous effort. "Most of our members come from grassroots organizing," Dailey says.

> When we go knocking on doors because somebody in that building called and said, "We're having problems. Will you please come over here and help us organize a tenants' association?" we may attract as many as 250 people to a neighborhood meeting. Our goal is not just to fix the immediate problem, but to find some people in that building who will emerge as community leaders; who'll stick around after the immediate issue has been settled. Then we try to recruit the cream of all these association leaders to work together as a team to run the coalition.

Her animation as she talks vividly demonstrates her delight in making such progress happen. Describing how the work of the coalition has evolved, she says,

In our early years, we focused very much on antiarson work and were the catalysts for renovating apartment buildings. In the process, we helped create six community development corporations, which renovated several thousand units of housing, mostly remodeling and rehab, but also some new construction. Code enforcement became another area of emphasis, and under Mayor Koch we were able to get the city to target inspections in buildings we identified, instead of sending one inspector at a time in response to individual complaints. Unfortunately, that policy was changed when Giuliani took over, but we are now waiting for the city council to pass a law mandating the right of tenant petitions.

As the Coalition became well established, it also reached out beyond the boundaries of the Bronx. Realizing the underlying need to provide more affordable housing in New York overall, Dailey has played a major role in the formation of Housing First, a citywide coalition. She also serves on the board of the Association for Neighborhood Housing Development, a coordinating group of some eighty-five organizations that serves as both think tank and pressure group. As Dailey explains: "We have helped to form citywide and statewide coalitions to fight for more money for schools, better salaries, construction funds, though right now is a bad time to do that."

On the state level, the organization has for some years had a contract to run New York's "weatherization" project, which pays for improving energy efficiency by installing new windows, insulation, and better plumbing in buildings where at least two-thirds of the residents are low income.

This kind of governmental recognition is based on the coalition's track record not only in achieving physical improvements, but in bringing together a polyglot population. While there are still remnants of the once primarily Italian and Jewish population, the Bronx is now largely Hispanic and African American, with a leavening of recent immigrant groups. "It is the organizers' job," Dailey explains, "to bring neighbors together across the barriers that usually divide them—language, religion, ethnic background—so that they can act together to make their neighborhood a better place to live."

One of the most promising of these community-building efforts has been to cultivate youth organizing and leadership, and fighting graffiti is not their only contribution.

Alex Cross represents the youth organization on the coalition board. He says that he is a second-generation volunteer:

> My mom did some work with the coalition to save the Bronx Hospital, and she let me know about the youth program. I went to the office and found out it was all about empowering youth in our community. I felt a need to do this, so I joined and put my all into it. We've accomplished a lot so far. Right now our biggest issue is school overcrowding.
>
> At our monthly meetings, kids come in and tell us what's on their minds. We don't tell them what to do—we guide them and teach them about the rules of getting into organizing. We have some three hundred-plus members, but our core group is about forty. A little while ago we got them to go to a "hip hop rally" at city hall to protest the budget cuts for the schools. We got 'em to restore it—not all of it, but about three-quarters.

Laura Vázquez, now a staff youth organizer, got started as an intern. "If you can make it through those three months," she recalls, "you can make it as an organizer." Now, she says, she is working on safety and quality-of-life issues:

> There are still a lot of empty lots in the Bronx. Some of our neighborhoods have been able to turn them into playgrounds; in others they've started community gardens that the tenants in the building take care of. Also, a lot of kids were just hanging out, not doing anything. Some dropped out of school until they got into this type of work. Now they have a safe place to hang out and they feel, wow, I have a role in society. So they're taking on more responsibility, and they're going to be our leaders tomorrow.

But a big problem is all the rents rising, so we try to hook up the tenants and get them to go to meetings with city council members, for instance. Sometimes it's tough to get adults to come to meetings. But when a youth hits the door and talks personally, they're like, wow, if you guys are really involved in this, yeah, I'll come to a meeting. I want to support you guys. At first adults were kind of weird about working with the youth, but now it's like there is no meeting without youth.

### Priorities for Tomorrow

Exemplifying the adage that each solution brings the next set of problems, once the Bronx again became a viable residential ommunity, rents began to go up as much as 25 percent, forcing people to work at two or three jobs and driving out long-term residents, particularly senior citizens.

Again it was time to get the facts. Daily elaborates,

> What we found was that these rent hikes were allowed under a state capital improvement program, permitting rent hikes if owners installed new windows or repaired the roof. As we dug around some more, we found that all these buildings had recently been refinanced by Freddie Mac [the Federal Home Loan Mortgage Corporation]. The trouble was that they had been way overfinanced.

In fact, some one-third of the area's apartment buildings had received Freddie Mac loans, but the agency was not enforcing the good repair clause in the contracts. Instead, unscrupulous speculators were doing a shoddy job of maintenance. One building was in such bad condition that it was down to five tenants and, De La Rosa recalls, the drug dealers who infested it were so powerful that she had to ask the police to go with her when she visited them.

"It was just horrifying to think that a federal agency could be so totally irresponsible," De La Rosa says. By 1990, 167 Freddie

Mac buildings had defaulted on their loans and sixteen were being foreclosed. Still, the agency offered only vague promises.

Coalition members decided to confront chief executive officer Leland Brendel at his Washington headquarters, with Dalma De La Rosa once again on the front lines:

> We explained to [the Freddie Mac executives] that if they didn't do what they were supposed to do they'd lose their shirts. It did no good. They were still lending money like drunken sailors, and a lot of the landlords they were giving loans to couldn't pay them off. Then we realized that some of the religious groups in the community had money in Freddie Mac, so we collected their proxies and decided to go to Alexandria [Virginia], and confront them at their stockholders meeting.
>
> When they saw us, they got scared. They said, you can't come in here. So a bunch of us, myself with five other people, said: "We have proxies. You have to let us in." The rest of the group waited outside, chanting. When Brendel came in and saw us he changed several colors. They didn't expect us and they were not going to mention the money they were losing in the Bronx . . . . So we stepped in and told them what it meant for them to walk into our community, giving out loans right and left, leaving buildings in bad condition, then being foreclosed, and finally walk away and not care. "We're not the bad people," we said. "We're the people in the neighborhood who have to pick up the pieces. How can you give millions of dollars in loans without checking to see what kind of building you're giving your money to?"

At one of the most notorious Freddie Mac buildings, the court-appointed receiver used harassment tactics to drive out the remaining tenants, so a busload of volunteers descended on the office of a Freddie Mac director in nearby Stamford, Connecticut. That night Mary Dailey got a phone call. "The guy was really mad," she recalls. 'You people have to stop this sort of stuff,' he says." But the "stuff" worked: gradually Freddie Mac responded by hiring someone to inspect buildings; foreclosing on some for lack of repairs, and selling them to reputable landlords. This success was further proof that what Dailey calls "the hit" can work as a last resort.

The coalition used the same formula—careful research, polite petitions, followed by direct action if necessary—to address the problem of class size in the schools. The need arose because the local school district was the third-most overcrowded in the entire city. Once again, as Dailey explains, the approach was fact-based and people-implemented:

> We started by first making sure the district was doing everything it was supposed to do and working with the local school board before advocating at the city board of education. We made sure the district had a good list of locations for new schools; then checked whether it jibed with the list of the central board. Then we decided to cut through all the middlemen and went straight to the chancellor, eventually bringing 100 parents to a meeting. We also met with the governor's appointee to the School Construction Authority and got the city comptroller to tour a school that was way behind in its construction schedule. Then, to get media attention, we got the City Advocate to come and hold a press conference together with the borough president. It helped that all three of these guys were running for mayor!
>
> We also had a lot of local mobilizations, marches, and rallies. What we proposed was that they turn an old armory into an education campus for a middle school, a small high school, and an athletic facility for a lot of local schools that don't have them. We held a major demonstration at the armory, people coming from all directions. It got a lot of coverage, in both the local and metropolitan papers.

One step forward and one step back. In 2002, with high hopes of winning the armory battle, the coalition had to mobilize to keep the board of education from busing seven hundred black and Hispanic kindergartners and first graders from a local public school to unfamiliar territory, in order to reduce congestion in a nearby affluent area. The plan was defeated, but the powers that be were slow to absorb the lesson that the area's working class would no longer permit itself to be dumped on.

## Dedication and Persistence

Asked to reflect on her years as coalition president, De La Rosa says, "You go to all the meetings, you go to board meetings in all the neighborhoods, you make sure things are going correctly and are available for whatever they need you for." She continues,

> We never asked anybody to do anything we weren't willing to do for ourselves. We didn't wait for somebody to come and clean our street; we went out and cleaned it. We did not say, come and rehabilitate our building unless we were willing to create a nonprofit housing company and help with the work.
>
> The reward has been the difference it's made in my neighborhood. Before the coalition went to work, in my neighborhood, the Crotona neighborhood, if you walked in that area you'd see a vacant building on your left, a vacant and decimated building on your right. Today, you see refurbished buildings on both sides. You see new homes, gardens, parks. You see new pride in our community. Working with everybody; that's what makes it a community.

She adds a personal note that illustrates how the coalition has changed not only buildings but people:

> My husband is rather sick now. But I don't worry when I'm at work if he fell or tripped, because there are about forty eyes looking after him. They come and ask him, "I haven't seen you in a while. How are you doing? I heard you weren't feeling good." That's what working with the coalition has accomplished. We're an extended family of neighbors.

But the fight isn't over. The destruction of the World Trade Center on September 11, 2001, wiped out revenues designated for housing that were tied to Twin Towers leases. Also in the aftermath, the coalition made special efforts to forestall retaliatory actions against Muslim residents and brought two area mosques into its network. Another setback was the election of a mayor with whom the coalition had not established close ties. This meant dealing with a commissioner of housing not willing to help with code enforcement.

Similarly, the switch from a board of education to mayoral control of the school system meant having to start with a new cast of officials who needed to be educated about the armory proposal. Research reports, one-on-one meetings, demonstrations, rallies, and visits to city hall—it's a never-ending effort.

To make matters worse, both New York State and City are now running record deficits that "present a situation where we can expect to see a major decrease in basic city services to our neighborhoods—in areas such as sanitation, parks, traffic, and senior citizen and youth service programs," Dailey reports.

That makes Veatch support ($25,000 in 2003) more vital than ever. Dailey adds,

> The policy of the coalition used to be to get funding from more mainstream and government sources. But government money keeps shifting and, anyway, is often so restrictive and requires so much paperwork that its value is questionable.
>
> When I tried to get a better match between what we were doing and our funding sources, Veatch was the obvious place to go. All my peers in organizations like ours know about Veatch. It's considered one of the prime sources of funding of community organizations like ours in the United States. They have a reputation of wanting to fund groups that are not just doing quality of life work but are trying to have a broader impact on changing social policy.

And there's something else. Getting Veatch support, more than that from any other source, is a sign of acceptance. It's like a seal of approval, and a big help when you apply to other funding sources.

Though a never-ending struggle, Mary Dailey and her staff of about twenty are tough and determined, seasoned by many battles. "I started in college as a student activist," she explained when asked to describe her motivation, "and when I graduated, I wanted to work on issues of economic and social justice." Moving to the Bronx because it was the cheapest place to live, she heard of an opening on the coalition staff. Rising steadily in the ranks, she remained there until 2005, when she resigned to join the Center for Community Change as a lead organizer. She is an inspiration not only for people in the Bronx but for everyone who shares her commitment to a fairer, more just society—making democracy work.

# Valley Interfaith
## *Making Colonias Part of the United States*

Connecticut Center for a New Economy and Alabama Arise define their "jurisdiction" as an entire state. The Northwest Bronx Coalition concentrates on one section of a major city. In Texas, Valley Interfaith takes as its purview a geographic area: the Rio Grande Valley of Texas or, more specifically, the valley's Mexican population. And once again women are in the forefront, both as staff and volunteers.

"For a long time our [state] legislators thought we were not part of Texas," says Acela Soza Garza, long-time Interfaith Valley volunteer and until recently a member of its executive committee. "What we've achieved since the late 1980s may not sound like a lot, but we're beginning to catch up with the rest of the state. They no longer think we're part of Mexico!"

Valley Interfaith, headquartered in Mercedes, is another volunteer-based but professionally supported coalition of the kind the Veatch Program singles out. For some twenty years it has been fighting for sustainable social and economic change—often with remarkable success. The story of how Acela Garza got involved is representative of its thousands of volunteers.

I belong to a church that's a member of the organization, and there was an announcement that some people would be going to Austin [the state capital] to work on health care. As a professional social worker who was born and raised in the Valley, healthcare has always been an issue for me, so I went with a group that was going to work on the indigent health care program.

We're only about six or seven miles from Mexico, and the decision makers were nowhere near the Valley and so paid no attention. We had no public hospital and no money for health care. In Austin, we talked to state senators and legislators and other decision makers and were able to get some state funds. . . . It wasn't all that much, but it was a beginning, and it showed us what community action could do.

"Leadership development is the cornerstone of Valley Interfaith's work," explains Sister Judy Donovan, until recently the group's lead organizer. For the last two years, an "Institutional Development" process among Valley Interfaith member churches and schools, led by trained teams of leaders, has sought, she says, "to expand the overall leadership base of the institutions, to build powerful core teams of institutional leaders, and identify key issues and action plans around those issues."

The Industrial Areas Foundation (IAF), the community self-help program inspired by Saul Alinsky, was instrumental in getting Valley Interfaith started.

Although he died in 1972, Alinsky is still a key figure in community organizing, having in a sense "invented" the movement when he launched Chicago's Back of the Yards movement in 1939. His "iron rule"—that organizers should never do for others what they can do for themselves—is still the guiding principle of IAF, and the Veatch Program has long been a key supporter. Marjorie Fine explains why:

There are more than 150 full-time professional IAF organizers, who staff more than sixty organizations in twenty states and the District of Columbia. IAF groups represent over three thousand congregations and associations with tens of thousand of ministers, pastors, rabbis, women religious and top lay leaders, unions, and civic leaders. All told, IAF groups represent virtually every faith, ethnicity, income level, and they come from across the political spectrum. As of 2003, the Veatch Program has invested close to $1 million in various IAF projects over the last twelve years.

As important as its economic victories is the IAF's legacy of developing strong leaders, transforming people from being passive and fearful and turning them into risk-taking leaders with the skills and talents necessary to reestablish a culture of democratic participation and accountability so sorely needed in our country.

The problems Valley residents tackled when IAF showed them how were staggering.

In 1983, some 220,000 people along the Mexican border in the lower Rio Grande Valley—half of them children—were living in colonias, unincorporated and unregulated communities. The rest of the state showed little awareness of their existence; officialdom considered them an embarrassment best hidden from press and public. Carmen Anaya, a Valley Interfaith leader, describes conditions this way in a 2000 report to the Ford Foundation:

> We didn't have lights, electricity; we didn't have sewers, we didn't have streets; we didn't have anything—nada, nada, nada. So I said, This is no way to live. Yes, I had these things, but all around me they did not. . . . I was worried about the children who didn't have any shoes, the children who walked a long way barefoot to get the bus to go to school. I saw all this and felt very sad for my people.

> Then the politics entered into it. The politicians were coming to my house. I'm telling you, Mrs. Anaya, that I'm going to bring water, I'm going to bring you lights, etc. Lying politicians. They came every month, the politicians with

their lies, until fifteen years ago. And the reason things changed was that Valley Interfaith arrived. . . . I learned with Valley Interfaith to be a leader.

By 1983, Valley Interfaith had gained enough strength to be able to get the then-governor and lieutenant governor to pay a visit. Gradually things began to change, as described by Eddie Anaya, second-generation leader in his family:

> Before people in the colonias did not have a voice and now they do. They have a sense of belonging to the democratic process, and they feel like, look, I count now…[and so they] go down to the local city commissioner's office and say, this is what we need because we're taxpayers, we're American citizens, and therefore we feel that we deserve the basics, which are water, sewer, lighting, and paving for our communities. More important, I think, is that we've been able to talk to each other, hear stories from each other, and build relationships with each other.

The passion of these volunteer activists won the respect even of officials on the receiving end of their efforts, such as Ed Archulta, general manager of the El Paso Water Utilities/Public Service Board:

> They've done a tremendous job here in El Paso County. In my opinion, they've been the movers and shakers to try to get the attention, to try to get something going. . . . I decided when I first met with them that it sounded reasonable to me for people that didn't have water or sewer services. . . . to get services.

## The Word Spreads

Even more important was the change in attitude of the local population. Elida Bocanegra was seven years old when she started working in the fields and she never went to school. Nonetheless, she was able to start a small local store. She says,

[When] I went out one morning to open my store, I saw the Colonia LaMesa flooded and the people and the children standing in front of my store on the highway…. And it came to my mind, "What should I do? These people need help." Nothing came to my mind because I didn't know nothing about nothing. The only thing I knew was working in the field.

One day a man went . . . to the store and he said, "Why are you so sad?" And I said, "That's because I don't know what to do. I don't know how to help these people over there." And he said, "Why don't you call Valley Interfaith?"

The first thing that came to my mind [was] "when I was a little girl, I needed some help, but nobody helped me. . . ." And I never quit. I just keep on doing it.

Her leadership in turn inspired others and perhaps, most important, Republican U.S. senator Kay Bailey Hutchison, who confirms,

The way I learned firsthand about colonias was Elida Bocanegra, who took me on a tour of my first colonia. And I will never forget the feeling that I had after walking through the mud and the sludge. . . . Valley Interfaith came to my office, and they said, "We want to work with you because we believe that you can do something." We have worked together and we've now put $300 million of federal money on the line for colonias in our country so that I will never walk through a neighborhood again that doesn't have clean water and sewer hookups. Never again.

But even with such support the battle for social justice is far from won. When government budgets are cut, help for the poor is invariably the first target.

Moses Robledo is the son of one of Interfaith Valley's original leaders. He was able to earn a university degree but returned to the Valley to help those left behind. There he discovered that the state

Water Development Board had frozen some $100 million of the moneys designated for Hidalgo County. Robeldo says,

> This was specifically money that was aimed at helping underdeveloped colonia areas with their septic tank, sewer connections ...
>
> I grew up near colonias. I have a lot of family and friends who lived in these areas. I knew the struggle they were going through, especially with flooding. When you're dealing with septic tanks, it's a problem because a lot of them overflow, and you have waste and whatnot, and it's a health hazard.
>
> A lot of people who live in the colonias don't have a college education. They don't have a public life, know-how. And Valley Interfaith has had years of experience and we're able to answer these people's questions.

Going to Valley Interfaith for information, he learned how to do research and develop connections. "The one thing that I really appreciate Valley Interfaith for is that I've learned to build relationships in public life," he says. "It's priceless."

Robledo is one of thousands of volunteers who, with the help of three staff organizers, have learned how to make the democratic process work. In 1995, the Texas legislature passed the last of a series of laws that made it unlawful to develop colonias without subdivision rules or infrastructure. Together with its allied organizations, Valley Interfaith has also succeeded in passing bond referendums that have brought nearly half a billion dollars in state and federal funding to the Valley, paying for water and sewer services for some 160,000 residents.

Such partnerships are vital, Sister Stephens points out, in developing and implementing statewide strategies. "All the organizations are independent," she continues, "but what we have in common is that we all have a contract with the Industrial Areas Foundation for leadership training and development and that we work together on common objectives."

For instance Valley Interfaith is involved in:

- The Valley Initiative for Development and Advancement (VIDA), a labor market intermediary that has trained thousands of residents for high-wage employment and set up Workforce Academies to prepare graduating high school students to pass college entrance exams.

- The Alliance School Initiative, which has organized hundreds of parents, educators, and community leaders to work together for higher student achievement and for the funds to make it possible.

- Achieving universal health care for children and state health care funding for the indigent.

Rosa M. Bodden, one of the volunteers who has worked on all these projects recalls,

> When Father Joseph O'Brian became pastor at my church, he started a relationship between our parish and Valley Interfaith. One Sunday after mass he announced that Valley Interfaith was having a meeting with [state] Senator Eddie Lucio in Harlingen. I went. What impressed me was seeing a hall full of leaders from churches throughout the Valley.

> At a training with Ernie Cortés [of IAF], I learned how the economy was connected to education, and that injustice exists within our economy here in the Valley. It was after this that I attended IAF national training.

> Education as my focus means the Valley Interfaith is my university. Whether I fight for services in the colonias, for better education through Alliance Schools, or for better job training through VIDA—I learn and develop as a leader.

## The Battle for a Living Wage

Sister Christina Stephens left the Valley in the late 1980s to head up IAF programs for the entire state. When she returned in 2003 to once again be the lead organizer for Valley Interfaith, she found matters much improved:

> When I left, we had to go city by city and colonia by colonia to get water and sewers. People were building their own homes out of cinder blocks. Now they are building really very nice subdivisions with water and sewer connections. That's certainly the result of the work that Valley Interfaith accomplished.

But while much has been gained, the root cause of the Valley's problems—persistent poverty—remains. The cliché has it backward: It isn't money but the *lack* of money that is so often the root of the evils in our society. So now, according to Sister Stephens, Valley Interfaith emphasizes living wage campaigns all up and down the Valley. This is a major struggle.

According to a March 2002 Valley Interfaith report,

> The Rio Grande Valley is home to one of the most impoverished workforces in the nation. Seventy-five percent of the overall Valley workforce earns poverty wages, while 39 percent of all Valley residents currently live in poverty. . . .
>
> This culture of poverty and low wages takes its toll on families. Unable to make ends meet, many working poor hold two to three jobs, making family life nearly impossible. Others become overwhelmed and turn to abuse or addiction. Children of these families, often left unsupervised, are more likely to turn to unhealthy behavior.

Valley Interfaith research turned up a fascinating fact: Nearly one-third of the Valley workforce was employed in the public sector—school systems, municipalities, counties—yet some 60 percent of them earned less than the federal poverty level. To implement its living wage strategy, the organization set out to see to it that no employee of school districts, cities, or counties was paid less than the federal poverty level for a family of four, which at the time was $8.49 per hour. The school districts were the first target.

Once again Acela Garza enlisted in the effort:

> The first school district we worked with was the McAllen district. We wanted the lowest-paid worker to get at least $7.50, knowing that that would automatically push those making more to a higher bracket. But we were very realistic; we did not expect them to do this overnight.

By using the well-learned tactics of house meetings to line up support and develop an agenda, then challenging school board candidates to take a stand at public meetings, Valley Interfaith soon scored some impressive successes; by 2000 the campaign had managed to raise the wages of 7,424 people.

Then, as Acela Garza recalls, came the backlash:

> The school districts were lifting wages, but then we began to hear horror stories of how managers were coming down hard on the employees. Cafeteria workers would be hounded, being told, for instance, that they had to clock out but keep working. They'd be told: "If you're not careful, you're not going to be here." And there was no entity that could help them. In Texas, you can't even *say* the word "union."
>
> So we began to organize Workers Associations, so that workers could begin to feel supported and know and understand their rights, so that they can't be intimidated. We're working very hard to find out just what the rights of workers are, so they can resist intimidating tactics without putting their jobs at risk.

To help support this ambitious effort, Valley Interfaith turned to the Veatch Program. As their year-end report to Veatch says,

> Valley Interfaith organized a clergy workshop on the Worker's Association strategy . . . [and] also organized 'Dignity of Work Sundays' in selected parishes to create space within churches for people to talk about their experience of work and to look for workers interested in building an Association. . . . Leadership development remains the cornerstone of Valley Interfaith's work.

## Democracy Is Catching

While tax-exempt organizations cannot take part in elections, they can and do educate voters about the issues, and that has repercussions.

Acela Garza tells the story of what happened in McAllen, a Valley city with a population of more than one-hundred thousand:

> Our notorious mayor had been in office for some twenty years. He had made his millions from the hundreds of acres he owned and the farm workers he employed. He was a very powerful man, well connected on both the state and national levels. He wanted a half-cent increase in the sales tax, but he wouldn't tell people what he would do with the money, so we came out against it and he lost. He came back the next year, and he lost again. The third time, he asked for our help. So we asked what the money was for and he was very ambivalent. So we said, we'll ask the people in the community and see what they want and then we'll negotiate.
>
> So we held hundreds of house meetings throughout the city and asked, "If you could decide what to do with $7 million, how would you want the money to be spent?" They said libraries, community centers, health clinics—things to meet human needs. We went to the mayor with seven agenda items and said if they were part of the referendum, we'd support it. Of course, he had his priorities, too—a golf course, money for a civic center—so we compromised. He got his golf course and we got our agenda items.
>
> A bonus was that the referendum brought out so many voters that the mayor, who was up for reelection, lost after twenty years.

With this victory to boost morale, the people of McAllen went after their next goal, single-district representation instead of city council members elected at large:

That was one of the most exciting times I've had in Valley Interfaith. We found it very difficult to hold the council members accountable to our issues, so we collected enough signatures to put our proposal up for a referendum. The power structure quickly raised $250,000 to campaign against us. We had all of $15,000—it was like David and Goliath. But we had learned how to get out the vote, so we concentrated not on campaign materials but on going door-to-door, explaining the issue, explaining the importance of every vote. We won!

Laughing happily at the recollection, Acela Garza comments,

That's the kind of success that keeps leaders like me going. It's a lot of work, but we know it benefits the community. Sometimes politicians don't give voters the credit they deserve. But when people are told about the issues, they'll vote for what they want. Then, once the candidates get elected, we spend a lot of time with them, pointing out what's important to our families.

On March 3, 2002, some two thousand Valley Interfaith delegates met with candidates for the U.S. Senate; for governor and lieutenant governor; for attorney general and comptroller, and for local offices. All were asked: Where do you stand on Valley Interfaith's agenda? To make sure they were listened to, Interfaith volunteers had prepared a "Sign Up and Take Charge" campaign that collected pledges from seventy-five thousand registered voters promising to go to the polls on election day. As a result, the *Dallas Morning News* reported voter turnout in the Valley was the highest in history. "Voting experts," the paper added, "attributed the large turnout to the get-out-the-vote effort by Valley Interfaith."

Such successes pay off in self-respect as well as in determination.

When Anastasia Ledesma and her husband moved to the colonia of Sparks in 1975, she was one of thousands who had no water and could find no way to obtain it. Then, as a leader of a Valley Interfaith sister organization, she started attending meetings of the Public Service Board (PSB). Finally, success seemed assured—but officials continued to treat valley residents with contempt. Ledesma reports,

> There was a meeting once with the PSB and they were getting very close to ensuring the water, but one of the officials in frustration yelled at us and said, "Well, you might get your water, but that won't make sure that you'll shower." That made me very sad that a public official would be responding to our needs in this way.

When she finally was able to turn on the tap in her house and water began to flow, Ledesma says, she "felt so overwhelmed by emotion that I just sat on the floor and cried." Now she had water, but she kept up her leadership role. "Maybe it's not going to benefit me directly, but I don't want people to have to go through . . . what I went through for so many years," she explains.

Carmen Anaya puts it this way:

> It is very fortifying to know that there is someone to train us to confront politicians. It is a university. And at the same time we are then able to educate others in order to think how to deal face-to-face with a politician and not humiliate ourselves or beg. We have the right to negotiate and tell him, "You are not our patron—you are our servant."

The politicians have also changed. Noelia Espinosa, now a high school teacher, recalls going to Austin to lobby for equalization of school funding:

> My representative said, "That's not going to happen. The rich districts are not going to want to give up their money. . . ."
>
> "Oh, but we're going to come and we're going to bring thousands of people to the steps," we said. And he said, "You can bring busloads, and it's not going to change."
>
> That was a lesson for him and he became very much our ally. Politicians don't expect to be challenged at a public meeting.

They expect to be lauded. They know better now. They do. They learn. They're not that dumb.

Sister Judy Donovan puts it more bluntly: "Now, politicians in the area either respect us or fear us. We don't really care which, as long as they work with us." As Acela Garza says, "They no longer think we're part of Mexico!"

# CAUSA
## *Working for Immigrants' Rights*

In August 2003, readers of New York City newspapers found a funny but troubling story about three young fishermen—the oldest twenty-one, the other two thirteen—who went out in an inflatable raft in Jamaica Bay and accidentally washed up at the edge of a runway of John F. Kennedy Airport.

After waiting anxiously to be picked up by a SWAT team, they went off in search of someone to report to. They walked the runways for seventy-five minutes until they found their way to the airport police station. Later the raft "captain" said: "You hear stuff about all these safety precautions and the terror alert being so high, and we're there walking around in an airport we didn't even know how we got into."

Not that then U.S. Attorney General John Ashcroft was unmindful of airport security. Under the label of Operation Tarmac, he busily rounded up immigrants who work for companies with airport contracts, even if they work at a distant location. By early 2002, 350 immigrants had been arrested, but not a single one was even suspected of any connection with terrorism. As the *Boston Phoenix* reported, "It's hard to imagine how the arrest and criminal prosecution of people who've done nothing worse than lie on a job application is going to make this country safer."

What it does do is make the lives of immigrants even more perilous and miserable. It is, as Ramon Ramirez of Oregon's CAUSA points out, also one more symptom of the problems his organization is trying to help solve:

> There is a lot of anti-immigrant sentiment and since 9/11 these people have been under extreme attack. In the state of Oregon alone, there have been twenty-one anti-immigrant bills introduced in the legislature. They range from barring people who are not citizens or legal residents from applying for a driver's license and requiring security guards to be U.S. citizens, to authorizing local law-enforcement agencies to cooperate more with the federal immigration service. That's on the policy level.
>
> On the economic level, employers are allowing immigration agents to search their records to see whether any undocumented aliens are working there. Operation Tarmac is one aspect of that. They're not only arresting airport screeners; if a company provides janitorial service . . . its janitors are subject to arrest even if they work 150 miles from the nearest airport. It's easy to scapegoat immigrants, so that's the kind of stuff we're having to fight off.

Another harassing maneuver began in 2002 when the Social Security Administration sent out "no match" letters to nearly one million employers, informing them of discrepancies, however trivial, between employment records and the Social Security database. The effect of these letters has been devastating, giving employers an excuse to fire affected immigrant workers—no one knows just how many—often because of their union activities.

CAUSA was started to fight for the rights of Latino and other immigrant families, primarily farm workers. In fact, Ramirez fills a dual role as coordinator of CAUSA and president of the farm workers' union.

The fruit and vegetable growers of Oregon's Willamette Valley have depended heavily on Mexican labor since the 1940s. Then, in the 1970s, reforestation work and plant nursery jobs emerged as major winter occupations. The obvious advantage for the workers was that, unlike seasonal employees in other states, they could obtain year-round employment, but winter and summer working conditions were equally miserable—long hours, low wages, no overtime pay or paid breaks, and no job security or other benefits. Often they are housed in squalid labor camps lacking basic sanitation, and even when they work with toxic pesticides, they are not always given proper protective gear or adequate training on how to use it.

In 1985, eighty workers got together to organize Pineros y Campesinos Unidos del Noroeste—The Northwest Treeplanters and Farmworkers United, or PCUN. The union now has more than five thousand registered members, of whom 98 percent are Mexican or Central American immigrants. According to Guadalupe Quinn, the organization's president, CAUSA was started eight years later when

> some people in Oregon became concerned about the anti-immigrant legislation that was being pushed in California, and realized that that was also likely to happen here. So we got together with human rights organizations, as well as unions and churches, to form a coalition that could keep an eye on what might happen on a state level. And that's what CAUSA is: a coalition.

> Ever since, we've continued to address the needs of farm workers and other immigrants, and also been concerned about what was happening to our students in the schools. Also, we realized that we couldn't limit ourselves to issues in the Latino community or to immigration issues, but that we had to help other communities of color that were facing problems, as well as women who're not being treated fairly, and people who're being ripped off at work. In fact, we have also reached out to our brothers and sisters across the border, because what happens here also has an impact on them.

In pursuit of these objectives, CAUSA, like so many other Veatch grant recipients, seeks to build coalitions with other organizations committed to social change and economic justice.

On the federal level, for instance, CAUSA has supported the "One Million Voices for Legislation" campaign which seeks to legalize the status of undocumented aliens. In October 2002, a million postcards in support of such legislation were delivered to President Bush and Congress—but more than a year later, nothing had been done.

## A Network of Unity

Given the enormity of the challenges, says Ramirez, CAUSA is working hard to make its supportive coalition grow, citing these examples:

> Recently we sponsored the People of Color Legislative Action Academy, bringing together leaders of the NAACP, the African American and Latino-Hispanic legislative roundtables, the Commission on Hispanic Affairs, and others. We brought in about 125 community leaders from around the state, training people in advocacy skills and having them discuss the top issues facing people of color.

> Meanwhile we continue to identify community organizations, including church groups and student organizations, to enlist in pushing our agenda. We are like a needle, weaving all these groups together so as to build a network for mutual support, for sharing resources so that newer groups don't have to reinvent the wheel, and in general to build a network of unity.

> In addition, we are participating in building a Northwest Immigrant Rights Coalition, made up of Oregon, Washington, Idaho, and Utah, starting with a conference in Boise. All these states have great budget problems—Washington, Oregon, and Idaho have millions of dollars in deficits—and the immigrants are being blamed for these economic and political crises. It's another example of scapegoating.

Altogether, some three hundred delegates gathered in Boise, and many of them went on to participate in the Immigrant Workers Freedom Ride in September and October 2003. Inspired by the Freedom Riders of the 1960s, more than nine hundred bus riders from forty-one states, representing some fifty nationalities, traveled a total of twenty thousand miles to present their case in Washington.

The ride had three primary objectives: to legalize the status of undocumented aliens and clear their path to citizenship; to reunite their families; and to gain the full protection of American civil rights and liberties for everyone, including fair treatment on the job. Forty-seven delegates, including Guadalupe Quinn, rode the bus from Oregon; they included immigrants from Mexico, the Philippines, and Russia, together with union workers and youth activists. One family brought along their five-year-old; the oldest rider was seventy-six. Like all the state delegations, they made numerous stops along the way to rally support. In Quinn's words,

> We stopped in thirteen places and met wonderful people everywhere we went—people of many different backgrounds coming together and recognizing that in order to create the change we need to solve our problems we really need to come together.
>
> There were workers, immigrants, young and old, regardless of religion, regardless whether they were victims of racism or homophobia. That to me was really important, because even ten years ago, people were working in their own communities, focusing on what affected them, and it was hard to bring even people of color together. Historically, they thought racism was only a matter of black and white. We didn't think how it also affected Latinos, Native Americans, or Asians.
>
> To me that was the most exciting thing about the trip.

Mary Martinez of the Network for Immigrant Justice, another Oregon delegate, kept a journal of the trip, in which she describes a typical local reception:

When we arrived in Omaha, we had a police escort to ensure our safety. The United Food and Commercial Workers union had been very active in organizing an evening program and dinner at the Martin Luther King Memorial Park. The mayor of Omaha opened the program and emphasized Omaha's rich history of immigration and the many contributions of Omaha's newest wave of immigrants. At each event we attended, different riders shared their personal stories. In Omaha, one of our *companeras* inspired and moved us as she told of her experience of religious persecution in Siberia. She sought political asylum in the States, at the expense of indefinite family separation. She provided an example of how bad immigration policies harm good people . . . and once again reminded us why were are in this struggle and the importance of the Freedom Rides.

Other officials who greeted them, she reports, included the president of the Denver city council, who told them that the council had adopted a resolution endorsing the ride; the mayors of communities from Rupert, Idaho, and Columbus, Ohio, to Washington, D.C.; as well as the governor of Iowa and his wife. At each stop, there were speeches by top labor and civil rights leaders. Admitting that after a while she felt as if she could recite them by heart, Martinez realized that one of the major objectives of the entire enterprise was to reach the local media in the communities they stopped in, so the repetition was well worthwhile. And wherever they stopped, they marched, chanting "Immigration built this nation!" and, over and over, "Si se puede" (We can do it). After two days in Washington meeting with their congressional representatives, the delegates went on to multiethnic Queens County, New York, where they were met by more than seven hundred buses carrying additional supporters. Among those attending the rally were three representatives of the Unitarian Universalist Service Committee, as well as local Unitarian Universalists coming by subway and car.

Not everything went smoothly. In Reno, riders were met by anti-immigrant demonstrators. But the scariest encounter took place outside El Paso, Texas, where immigration officials boarded two of the Los Angeles buses and threatened the riders with arrest and deportation. One of the photos that made it into the Sunday *New York Times* shows a passenger holding up a sign that reads, in part, "I wish to exercise my right to remain silent. I will not speak to anyone, answer questions, respond to accusations, waive any of my legal rights, or consent to any search of my person, papers, or property until I have first obtained the advice of an attorney." One of the union organizers on the bus was reminded of the time when, as a high school senior in 1959, she and other black students tried to integrate her high school, and whites in her Dallas suburb tried to stop them by throwing rocks and firecrackers.

This time there was no violence, but the three-hour stand-off didn't end until church and union leaders and even members of Congress intervened with the Bush administration.

A significant aspect of this immigrants' demonstration was that organized labor was a major financial supporter, and John J. Sweeney, president of the AFL-CIO, gave a speech in which he said, "Injustice anywhere is a threat to justice everywhere." For many years the labor movement had a reputation of being hostile to immigrants on the assumption that they were stealing jobs from union workers. But by the 1990s, this attitude began to change as labor leaders realized how much of a stake in simple justice native-born and immigrant workers have in common. In addition, the labor movement, steadily shrinking in numbers, needed to organize the newcomers if it was to retain its influence and power.

Still, as Bishop Nicholas DiMarzio of Brooklyn told the Queens rally, "The way immigrants have been treated is a blot on the nation's conscience. . . . This must stop and this immoral system must be changed."

## Fifty Years Later

From the perspective of more than two decades fighting for immigrant rights, Quinn considers what has been happening recently, both locally and nationally, as particularly challenging. "There's been a lot of pressure from the growers to take away some of the gains the farm workers won through their union," she says.

> I'm an immigrant myself. My parents came here in 1951 when I was three, and I'm afraid that things haven't changed all that much from what they had to struggle with fifty years ago.
>
> Not only do we still have a long way to go, but in some ways we may be going backward. Back then there wasn't all that blatant anti-immigrant stuff that's come up in the last few years. One experience that made me realize that we're not in a better place was visiting some of the farm workers' housing with a group of church people in 1999. What I saw just made me want to cry. I stood there realizing that their living conditions were worse than what I remember from when I was growing up. There were eighty or so people living in a place without running water and with only one bathroom. I don't remember anything like that.

But, while appalled and discouraged, she is not willing to give up. In fact, she says, that's what keeps her going:

> For me, CAUSA is very significant, in the sense that we're aware of what is going on, and that—with the help of a lot of good allies—we're doing everything we can to mobilize folks so they can take care of themselves. That's the key: not fixing their problems for them but developing leadership at the grassroots level so they can fix them themselves.

Reflecting on the Freedom Ride she adds,

> The real work begins now that we're home. We still need to educate people about the need for immigrant justice, but I feel stronger for having been on the ride. Not only did I develop some great friendships during twelve days together on the bus, but we formed some much stronger coalitions with all the other folks from Oregon and with other organizations on the national level. That was the most exciting

thing—discovering this wonderful coalition of people everywhere we went, seeing community after community ready to enlist to help each other and to care about each other.

Martinez says she came to the same conclusion:

One thing is clear: the Freedom Riders have contributed to building a new coalition that must continue to mobilize immigrants, faith communities, labor, community organizations, and students in a unified way in behalf of immigrant justice. We have confidence that we can do it.

And she signs off with a ringing affirmation of the Freedom Riders' slogan: "*Si se puede!*"

# Pacific Institute for Community Organization
## *Developing Community Leadership*

JIM KEDDY, DIRECTOR of the Pacific Institute for Community Organization's California Project, first became an activist for social justice when he was a college student. Two causes engaged his allegiance, fighting apartheid in South Africa and the oppression of the poor in Central America. His commitment has never weakened. After graduation he joined the Peace Corps and worked as an educator under the auspices of the Costa Rican Ministry of Adult Education, which assigned him to a border community populated by many refugees from war-torn Nicaragua. It was a community with severe disease and sanitation problems and no running water.

The ministry, he recalls, "had adopted a model based on the philosophy of Brazilian educator Paulo Freire who, in such books as *Pedagogy of the Oppressed*, argued that literacy education for adults should not be just about reading, writing, and arithmetic. Instead, it should also help them learn to analyze conditions in their community so they understand what's at the root of their problems, to move them from being spectators to being active participants." Keddy was fascinated by that approach, he says, and began to do some simple organizing in addition to his teaching.

Returning to the United States in 1987, he enrolled at the Graduate Theological Union (GTU), the interdenominational seminary in Berkeley, California. (One of its constituents is the Unitarian Universalist Starr King School for the Ministry.) "I wanted to continue to work in the area of adult education and social change. While overseas, I had also developed a strong interest in theology and faith, and I wanted to see if I could combine these interests by getting a master's degree at GTU," Keddy explains.

While doing his graduate work, Keddy also attended some PICO meetings in nearby Oakland. He was impressed by the way the people who were being helped assumed leadership roles, running meetings and making decisions. "I realized that leadership development drives everything else when it comes to effecting social change. It also struck me that this was happening in a faith-based context and that it helped local congregations to live up to their values and mission. I immediately got hooked on this approach," Keddy concludes. He's been hooked ever since, serving not only with the California Project but as a director of the national PICO (pronounced "peakoe") network.

Founded in 1993, the California Project embraces seventeen affiliated organizations, each governed by a local board of religious and community leaders. The number keeps growing, sometimes through the initiative of local clergy and sometimes with the help of the state leadership. Community priorities are determined by local initiative, and together the affiliates address statewide issues that affect them in common. The California Project is widely regarded as the best organized, most effective progressive organization working in the state's policy arena. As Gail Lang, one of its volunteers, puts it, "We can do anything. We have the process, we have the people, we have the passion, and we have the pain. We can do anything."

## Big Victory for Smaller Schools

Its success in the field of education is a good example of what PICO has been able to achieve. In 1997, the Sacramento affiliate decided to concentrate on improving its local schools, which tended to be ethnically mixed and poorly performing. Often parents did not speak English as a first language, and there was, according to Keddy, "a real disconnect between the families and the school staff":

> Teachers felt that they were not being supported by the families and tended to blame the parents for what was going wrong. The parents, on the other hand, felt completely left out. We took a look at what it would take to change this situation, and found that a very small number of teachers were successfully using home visits to build relationships.
>
> We developed a pilot project with eight schools; then were able to get the school district to launch a new program that would pay teachers to carry out home visits. We found that these visits not only got parents more involved but also helped teachers to have a better understanding of the family situations and culture of their students. It was so successful that it took off like wildfire.

PICO quickly decided to apply the Sacramento model to other communities, getting the legislature to fund a statewide program of teacher home visits, and by 2003, some six hundred schools in California had received grants to support such programs. "One thing that has surprised us," Keddy adds, "is how much teachers like it," because they are getting far better support from parents and there are fewer blame situations. PICO believes that no other state has a program like California's. The only other effort to make home visits part of the educational process is the Head Start program, but in California it involves all grades—middle, high, and elementary schools.

Meanwhile, PICO's Oakland affiliate continues to tackle the problems of its big and badly overcrowded public schools. One elementary school built for six hundred students, for instance, now has an enrollment of fourteen hundred, but progress is being made. Within two years, nine new, smaller schools were created. Applying its strategy of replicating what works, PICO is now trying to spread this model throughout California, with both its San Jose and Sacramento organizations working hard to create new, smaller schools.

As of 2001, unfortunately, much of PICO's energies have had to be devoted not to achieving new victories but to keeping old ones from being diluted or dismantled. This is a trend that has hit virtually every state in the nation, as the economic downturn abruptly started a cycle of growing deficits, with California's budget crisis making national headlines. But while other states tried to balance their budgets through drastic cuts in social and welfare appropriations—tax increases having become the great political taboo—California's legislature at least at first restored many of the proposed massive cuts.

PICO made the difference.

Jim Keddy explains, "We brought four thousand leaders together at a statewide town hall meeting in Sacramento to propose some positive options for the state budget and to protect vital services for families in health care, education, and housing." It was another example of PICO's strategy of bringing the collective voices and concerns of diverse low- and moderate-income Californians to the statewide policy arena on issues of common interest.

## Taking Advantage of the Democratic Process

Demonstrating that direct democracy can help support progressive as well as reactionary causes, the voters in November 2002 approved a PICO-supported $2.1 billion bond issue for affordable housing. Following up on this success, the state organization encouraged its affiliates to meet with local housing developers. As Keddy points out,

It's one thing to win a budget or policy victory. It's a whole different thing to have it translated into real change at the local level. When we make an effort to fight for something at the state level, we try to follow up with the second step, which is to make sure that the local communities benefit from the change. That's why when we won funding increases for health clinics, we then tried to make sure that the local community clinics applied for the grants.

The same way we're now trying to make sure that our affiliates capture as much of that housing bond money as possible. That's especially important because budget cuts have stripped almost all of the money for affordable housing out of the state's general fund. It's all part of our continuing effort to create positive synergy between our local organizations and what we're doing on the state level.

In any political environment, the healthiest dynamic is to have local activities and state activities on a policy level going on at the same time—one feeding the other. And the common denominator at both levels is that the vast majority of the work is being done by volunteers, not by staff. Our organizers function primarily as trainers and coordinators. In fact, there are only four people on our state staff, but when necessary those four and the local organizers function together to promote our statewide programs.

At all levels, PICO is directed by volunteers, with staff providing only supporting and training functions. The best training of all, however, comes from experience, as when volunteers chair meetings, meet with legislators, hold press conferences, and testify at Capitol hearings.

Like his counterparts in other Veatch-supported organizations, Keddy stresses the twin objectives of solving immediate problems and making the democratic process work. As Keddy puts it,

Democracy is not something that happens only in elections. Voting counts, but it's a very limited way of thinking about citizenship. It has to happen all the time since only continuous political action creates the power to change systems. In fact, it often works the other way around: that once people who are not registered get involved in a local issue that directly affects them, once they see the difference they can make by working in their own community, then they go out on their own initiative to register and vote. If we are going to be the most productive society possible, we need people from all sectors to be engaged in debate about public policy.

## The National Scene

PICO's national director is a Jesuit priest, Father John Bauman, who started organizing in the 1960s in Chicago, then put his organizing skills to work in Oakland in the early 1970s. Since then, PICO has grown from a small, local organizing project to a national network, considered so effective that Interfaith Funders picked it as one of only five organizations to receive grants to study organizer recruitment—the biggest key to starting additional community organizations and making sure they succeed.

What has made PICO so effective at establishing itself in new communities is its five-step strategy. First it raises seed money for a feasibility study. Then it recruits a core group of local volunteers. The third step is to assist these volunteers in creating a sponsoring committee made up of local religious and community leaders which oversees the initial organizing effort and seeks to establish a secure base of local funding. Only then does the national staff take a leading role by hiring and training a paid organizer.

The fruit of these efforts, as described in the PICO web site, is that

people learn to participate in and influence our political system and democratic institutions. Those who were previously ignored, excluded, or apathetic become involved. People's stake in our society is made real. Family life is strengthened.

The once-torn fabric of neighborhoods and communities is rewoven. At the very heart of this mission is the process of helping people to help themselves.

The statement goes on to say that congregations of all denominations provide the foundations of the PICO community organizations because they come together "in a powerful expression of unity that transcends racial, ethnic and income differences," based on three common principles: *respect for human dignity, creation of a just society, and development of the whole person.*

## Affirming Core Values

Keddy admits that religion can be used for narrow, sectarian purposes, for antisocial ends. However, he continues, movements for justice in this country—the abolition movement, the early labor movement, the civil rights movement—share a history of combining the traditions of discipleship and citizenship. By contrast, "when people act only in their own interest in the public arena, citizenship can come down to a sort of lowest common denominator, fighting only for a single, limited cause."

Without minimizing the importance of the support PICO receives from many faith traditions, Keddy speaks warmly of the role played by Unitarian Universalist congregations and individuals, and particularly by the Veatch Program. He calls Veatch "probably the best money in the whole country for community organizing. Not the biggest, but the best." Most foundation money is tied to specific issues, he explains. Some fund healthcare programs, others emphasize education reform, "but the money that supports social justice is very small. Most foundations are very leery of community organizing. There's Veatch, Interfaith Funders, the Catholic Campaign for Human Development, and a handful of others. We depend heavily on those few and are most grateful for their support."

PICO's "stunning successes," in the words of the *San Diego Union-Tribune*, owe more to the enthusiasm and commitment of thousands of volunteers than they do to money. Volunteer Mary Schlarb of Alameda County comments,

> People who thought that their word didn't mean anything to anybody see that by coming together we can make a difference. Our voices are heard. We see that we are not powerless. We have a part in this government and that is exciting."

Jose Guadalupe Tinajero of Orange County echoes that sentiment: "Before we started organizing, we did not have a voice. People who were suffering and people who were poor, they did not have hope. Now we have a voice. We have respect."

"We are a representation of what America is all about, democracy at work. We make things happen," says Liza San Andres of San Mateo County. And LaCresia Hawkins of Stockton sums up volunteers' motivation:

> We do this because of our faith. When you are out there in the community, you see people's pain. And you see that if you don't keep working, keep fighting, it's not going to get any better. I look back at all we've won, and I know that I just have to keep going. I can't stop now.

Volunteers like these are the building blocks underlying PICO's success. Money is the cement.

# The Association of Community Organizations for Reform Now
## *Empowering the Poor*

WHEN DAVID EVERETT wrote in 1791 that "tall oaks from little acorns grow," he couldn't have been thinking of the Association of Community Organizations for Reform Now (ACORN). But the metaphor inspired the welfare mothers in Arkansas who got the organization started. And grow this little acorn did: It is now generally recognized as the largest low- and moderate-income membership organization in the United States, with more than six hundred "branches"—the neighborhood chapters that work on local and statewide issues. Combined, they have a membership of more than 120,000 families.

Usually when a new chapter is formed, the first (by now familiar) step is for organizers to knock on doors and ask the residents what would improve their lives. Invariably, housing, jobs, education, and health care top the list. Fair lending practices are not far behind, and might rank even higher if people understood how they are being victimized by predatory creditors. ACORN organizers then show them how, by joining together, they can obtain the help that is beyond their reach as individuals.

To show how a local affiliate operates, Ann Sullivan, executive director of Long Island (NY) ACORN gives this example of a woman in Roosevelt, one of the pockets of poverty in generally well-to-do Nassau County, who had been renting a house that was barely within her means:

> One day the landlord showed up to tell her he didn't want to rent to her any more—but he was willing to sell. "I can't buy it," she said. "I don't have that kind of money." He told her not to worry, that her monthly payment would be no more than her rent. "What about taxes and insurance?" she asked. "It's all included," he told her.
>
> She couldn't get him to show her the papers beforehand, so she went to the closing and signed, but since her first language is Spanish it wasn't until after she got home that she figured out that the monthly payment was $300 more than her rent. Then she discovered that taxes and insurance were not included, so she came to us, and when we looked at her documents we found that she not only had a 14.7 percent mortgage, but there was a balloon payment of $155,000 at the end of fifteen years, and that she'd been charged an $8,000 broker's fee. Well it's hard enough to make ends meet if you have a decent mortgage, but if you've been cheated that brutally you're wiped out. No wonder we have so many foreclosures in our neighborhood.

Long Island ACORN follows a two-prong strategy to cope with such problems. First, it offers loan counseling to help people understand predatory lending practices, such as upfront payments for premium credit insurance at outrageous rates to skirt state usury laws. But that is not enough, which is why the second prong requires going after the companies that victimize them:

> There was a branch office of a national loan company just around the corner from our office, which made it easy to get a delegation to stand outside, picketing and chanting. The manager came out and said, "Oh, we don't do that kind of thing." One of the victims was right there and yelled, "Oh, yeah?" We had alerted the media, and they interviewed her at her house, and the next time she went to pay her mortgage, the manager

said: "Mrs. Fisher, I understand we made a mistake on your mortgage, but I'm going to take care of that right away."

A happy ending, except that these problems cannot be solved on a case-by-case basis. Since mortgage companies such as Household Finance and Beneficial are beyond the reach of local or state chapters, that's where national ACORN comes in. The Nassau chapter joined with other affiliates from all around the country to tackle the company at its corporate base. Here, according to Sullivan, is what happened next:

> We went to the Household Finance headquarter in Chicago, and then to the houses of board members. We put up big signs on their lawns that said, "Foreclosed for Moral Bankruptcy," and we left flyers with their neighbors with a picture of the guys that said: "Watch out. You've got a loan shark in your neighborhood. "

This kind of coordinated effort plus legal intervention by national ACORN headquarters resulted in a record settlement of $480 million paid to abused customers, but such tactics are not generally considered "nice" and make it tough to get mainstream foundation funding. The Veatch Program, which is not afraid to tackle controversial issues, has provided essential support for both the national ACORN organization and some of its local chapters.

Veatch offers its grant recipients another great advantage: It is flexible enough to be able to respond to unscheduled opportunities and to offer emergency grants without a lengthy, bureaucratic process. For example, in the 1990s a subcommittee of the House Banking Committee voted to exempt some 80 percent of the banking industry from a law intended to encourage mortgage loans to the poor.

The day the full committee was scheduled to vote, the lobbyists, as is their practice, paid so-called couriers to hold places in line as early as 2 AM to make sure the bankers' representatives would get seats at the hearing. But when the placeholders got there, they found to their amazement that someone had beaten them to it. Even at that early hour, the steps of the Capitol were crowded with still earlier arrivals, and when the doors opened, the room was quickly filled not with the expected supporters of the repeal legislation but with folks with a firsthand stake in defeating it. These early arrivals were ACORN members who had come by bus from as far away as Chicago.

The banking lobbyists were not pleased. This legislation, one of them complained, was at the top of their priority list. And they had further reason to be disappointed when the full committee voted to reject the gutting amendment. ACORN had managed to respond promptly to the subcommittee vote by turning to Veatch for a special grant to help pay for the buses.

## Early Victories

The struggle against predatory lending is not likely to ever end, especially if business interests succeed in convincing Congress to pass toothless federal legislation that preempts state laws. Other issues, however, can sometimes be resolved just by exposing them to the light of public scrutiny.

Long Island ACORN has several such successes to its credit. One of them seems almost trivial, but it happened early in the group's history and thus gave it instant credibility with a broad swath of the population. When the New York Metropolitan Transportation Authority introduced its electronic fare system, called MetroCard, riders were promised free transfers from MTA buses to the New York City subway. "But when passengers from Nassau County got to the Jamaica transfer station, they found that the people who had got on the bus in Queens got the free transfer, but people from Nassau had to pay an extra $1.50," Ann Sullivan recounts. "So the Long Island ACORN members got together and complained. Within a few days then Senator D'Amato held a press conference to say Long Islanders should have free transfers, too, and the MTA agreed. People were really excited about winning that fight."

Another success, she continues, was triggered by a bad fire in a building that housed many subsidized tenants who had had some ACORN media training:

> The landlord did only a little bit of repair, so the tenants held a meeting in the lobby, and the superintendent said, "You can't meet in the lobby. The landlord doesn't want you to." So they said, OK, you've got a job to do—call the police. But they also called the local cable channel and the papers, and after that publicity the mayor toured the building, and after that the repairs started happening in a big way.

Housing remains a big issue. In one instance, ACORN did some digging and found that one landlord owned several substandard buildings that he was renting primarily to Latinos because, according to Sullivan, landlords think they can easily run over them. But once again, the tenants—ACORN-taught and media savvy—and with a bit of luck, prevailed. Sullivan explains,

> We got some fifty or sixty tenants to come to a village hall meeting to demand the mayor tour the buildings. Finally, he came out on a Tuesday afternoon, and he was annoyed that we'd got the press there. We showed him ceilings falling down but he just kept complaining about overcrowding. The press was just about to leave when the landlord's son showed up, and the first thing he did was to try to shove the reporters off his property.
>
> Then he got in the mayor's face: "Is there a problem?" Well, the mayor didn't like that and he said: "You telling me to leave?" By now the mayor is spitting mad and he gets on his cell phone to call the police. At that point the landlord's son decides to leave and he jumps in his car and the driver tries to take off. Just then four police cars come roaring up . . . and cops come running from two directions and pull the landlord's son out of his car and put handcuffs on him. Meanwhile the tenants spontaneously start chanting "The people united will never be defeated." That night and throughout the week it's

all on local television, and the mayor was so mad he assigned one building inspector just to go after this guy's buildings.

These events galvanized the community, a low-income area heavily populated by African Americans and Latinos who were used to having their rights trampled on and having their complaints ignored. The tenants had been afraid to go after the landlord because he was known for sending in thugs and people had been beaten in the alleyways. Now, emboldened by the experience of success, people no longer feel helpless, and they know that some half-dozen Long Island ACORN organizers stand ready to offer counsel, help plan strategy, do background research, and give them media and organizing training.

## Teaching School Boards a Lesson

Never was such help more important than when some Long Island minority communities decided to tackle their uncooperative school boards. The problems were basic. Kids were not being taught to read; their math skills were abominable. When ACORN began to gather the facts, it turned out that in Hempstead—and the same pattern prevailed in Baldwin and Uniondale and Garden City—of about five hundred kids who started high school only some one hundred and fifty graduated, and of those only a pitiful three received the kind of diplomas required to qualify for college. They also found that Latino kids were not being given homework. The attitude seemed to be, "Well, they don't speak English so they're not going to learn anything anyway."

So ACORN trained parents to call their schools and ask: How many kids are in the school? How many per class? What courses are offered? Then the staff compared these numbers with statewide averages. Ann Sullivan describes one of the devastating statistics they uncovered:

> We found out that state requirements called for ninth graders to be offered a math sequence that would qualify them for a Regents diploma. It turned out that in Hempstead there were

eleven such sections—but only one was actually being taught at the Regents level. The other ten were a sham. That meant these kids could never pass the exam that qualifies you for a Regents diploma. So we issued a report that we called "Documenting a Disaster," which we launched at a big press conference.

We followed that up by asking for a meeting with the superintendent of schools. He said yes, but would never set a date. Then we started dogging them at budget hearings, so what they did was to call the meeting to order and then immediately go into executive session. Then they'd meet behind closed doors for three or four hours. Well, how many parents can sit around that long to finally have their say? Not only that, but they started to move school board meetings around and changing the date at the last minute, so parents couldn't figure out when and where they were meeting.

We sent postcards to the school board president demanding they schedule meetings ahead of time as required by the state open meeting law, and we sent flyers to all the president's neighbors saying: do you know what your neighbor is doing? After a while, those tactics began to work, and we now have regular school board meetings with a time at the beginning when the public can have a say.

## The Battle Never Ends

This was all good practice for perhaps the greatest showdown yet.

The scene, again, is the village of Hempstead, where a department store building had stood empty for many years. Then Hempstead launched a major redevelopment plan. The department store was torn down to make room for the "big box" retailers, Home Depot and Stop & Shop. But the plan also called for tearing down three apartment buildings as well as some dozen private homes. By publishing the required notices, not in *Newsday*, the well-read county paper, but in a paper with a tiny circulation available only by mail, the authorities tried to keep these plans secret. Ann Sullivan describes the rest: "Somebody gave us a heads up about the public hearing and in three days we turned out about 125 people." They were mostly Spanish speaking and, though the meeting was conducted in English, the ACORN folks were not intimidated. Again and again they stood up to ask for a translator until finally, Sullivan reports, one was provided:

> That was the beginning of a campaign that went on for two years. They kept telling us they had a relocation plan. We demanded they show it to us, and it turned out to be nothing more than a retyping of the federal laws requiring a plan, but no indication where the seventy-five or so families were going to go—all in the midst of an incredible housing shortage, with people walking into our office every day pleading for an apartment.
>
> We decided to organize a clergy breakfast, where the people in these buildings told their stories. The clergy members who were there got together to hold a prayer vigil, which helped to get more and more people to understand the issue and to increase the public pressure. Even so, the town managed to secure a $20 million loan from HUD [the federal Department of Housing and Urban Development], but it's a HUD mandate that there be a relocation plan. We went to the county and showed clearly that there was no relocation plan, so they never got their $20 million. All they got was about $4.4 million—just enough to pay the bills for what was already there, but not nearly enough to go through with the expansion. So eventually we won.

Illustrating the way one struggle feeds another, ACORN staff found out by talking to the mostly Latino families in the housing fight that their kids were not receiving an adequate education—which triggered a new battle.

## The Ripple Effect

As word of ACORN's victories spreads, so does its influence. More and more chapters are being organized in other parts of Long Island. The organizing pattern remains the same: knocking on people's doors, asking what they would like to see changed in their neighborhood. Okay, people are then told, to get those changes you'll have to get together. Will you come to a meeting? A few do and elect leaders who, in turn, meet with their counterparts from other chapters and hear reports of what can be accomplished. Given that encouragement, and staff help, they are ready to grow.

Once established, the new chapter combines with others to make decisions about issues that affect Long Island overall, such as cuts in bus service. This is what ACORN calls "coordinated autonomy." Then Long Island chapters meet with those in New York City, in nearby counties, and finally the whole state, whereupon state officers elect the representatives who will serve on the national board to help shape national policy.

The ACORN story illustrates how many Veatch Program grants achieve not just one but several Veatch objectives. As the program's 2002 annual report puts it: "We look for organizations that are developing new public policy and new ways of organizing from the grassroots." It then amplifies this underlying concept:

> We see the Veatch Program as helping to build a movement for social change. We focus not only on particular issues but also on the methods being used to address them. Does an organization involve its members in decision making? Does the pursuit of justice dictate the organizational practices as well as the organizational goals? Does it trust the grassroots and understand that political power does not come from opinion polls, but from a politically literate population that clearly understands the alternatives being presented? Does the organization work cooperatively with other organizations and seek to build a broader "civil society"?

As an essential part of rebuilding our democracy, the Veatch Program supports organizations that teach people the skills that have been lost as they have been systematically excluded from the political process: the skills of analysis, public speaking, conducting meetings, raising money, challenging bureaucrats, and holding political representatives accountable.

ACORN and its affiliates meet all of these criteria with courage and skill. Standing up at a public meeting to ask for a translator is only one small—but critical—example of the difference self-confidence can make.

# Ella Baker Center for Human Rights
*Putting Justice Back in the
Criminal Justice System*

To BE YOUNG, poor, and either black or Hispanic all too often means that you have incurred the proverbial "three strikes" and land in jail. The scope of this problem is why James Bell, a staff attorney for the Youth Law Center of San Francisco, said, "It is clear to me that incarceration will be the civil rights and human rights issue of the twenty-first century."

Here are a few figures to bolster his assessment.

The United States incarcerates a higher percentage of its population than any other nation that boasts of being civilized, and in 2002 the nation's inmate population set a record at 2.1 million. As a corollary, what critics call the "prison/industrial complex" has become a huge business. Prison spending has gone up over 800 percent in the last twenty years (while spending for higher education is down by roughly 20 percent), and the building of prisons is one of America's few growth industries. Between 1980 and 2000, California's prison population grew by 40 percent—in the face of a 55 percent drop in the crime rate. Also, California imprisons juveniles at double the rate of adults, and jails more kids than any other state.

Statistics put people to sleep, but here is one more bit of data that might wake us up. In 1997, California—and California is far from unique—spent an average of $5,327 per student in its school system, as opposed to $32,200 to house a youngster in one of its correctional facilities. And demonstrating just how powerful the prison lobby has become, when the state 2003 budget was in turmoil, prison guards were scheduled for a pay rise, while teachers were being laid off and allocations for parks, daycare centers, and public health programs were also being slashed.

The brunt of this tragic trend is borne by communities of color. When youngsters are arrested for drug offenses, black kids are forty-eight times more likely, and Latinos thirteen times more likely, to get locked up than whites.

The Ella Baker Center for Human Rights (EBC) is in the forefront of the struggle to combat these inequities. As its application for a Veatch grant says, it "documents, exposes, and challenges human rights abuses in the U.S. criminal justice system, and builds power in communities most harmed by government-sanctioned violence."

To achieve these objectives, EBC combines policy reform, media advocacy, legal services, and public education with grassroots organizing and direct action. Located in the San Francisco Bay area, it has achieved enough local successes to enable it to try to replicate its programs both statewide and nationally. EBC is named for a prominent leader of the 1960s civil rights battles, who said, "We who believe in freedom cannot rest until it comes."

Van Jones is EBC's founder and national executive director. After working as a reporter, editor, and graphic artist for several news organizations, he graduated from Yale Law School in 1993, and joined the Lawyers' Committee for Civil Rights in San Francisco. In 2002, Court TV honored him as one of seven African Americans under age forty who were making "significant and enduring changes in politics or the law." Among his many other honors, Jones has also been named a "next generation leadership fellow" by the Rockefeller Foundation, and one of fifty "human rights heroes" by Kerry Kennedy-Cuomo in her book, *Speaking Truth to Power.* Trim, slim, and dressed in fashionable black, he could well have chosen to become a fashion model rather than a role model in the human rights movement.

## Youth Activism

One of the messages he has been addressing to "power" is that young people need "Books Not Bars," and that is the name of a program the Ella Baker Center launched in 2001, which he is also heading nationally. It is, says Jones, "an effort to harness the continuing outrage at a criminal justice system that unfairly targets youth—mostly low-income youth of color—and an education system that fails them."

The outrage Jones refers to came to a boil when California voters were asked to approve a referendum that, in the words of EBC staff member Lenore Anderson, was intended "to push a huge number of kids into the adult criminal justice system." The implications, she points out, were doubly pernicious. For one thing, it made youngsters as young as fourteen liable to much longer sentences. An even bigger threat, she says, "is the permanency of the felony record that can determine their fate for the rest of their lives. Juvenile convictions can be sealed, but an adult sentence even at the age of fourteen means they will have to report it on job applications when they're fifty."

To fight this proposition, EBC supported a youth-led public education campaign that helped generate a wave of youth organizing under the banner of "Schools Not Jails." According to Jones,

> Many compared this upsurge of youth-led activism to the student-led sit-in movement that energized the civil rights struggle in 1960. The leadership of youth organizers and our coordinated media strategy provided the opportunity for hundreds of young people, many in high school, to speak directly to decision makers and the electorate about the negative impact that this new law would have on their lives.

Although the proposition was approved, the three counties that recorded a majority of "no" votes (Alameda, San Francisco, and Los Angeles) were the three where EBC led organized opposition and conducted active public education, with young volunteers going door to door.

This experience persuaded the EBC leadership to design strategies that would go beyond responding to single crises and look to more long-term solutions. That was the origin of the Books Not Bars program, which combines public education, technical support for youth organizations, media mobilization, policy advocacy, and research-based reports. The program is now going nationwide, but Jones explains why Oakland remains a main focus:

> Oakland is one of the cities most affected by the oppressive presence of the criminal justice system. A combination of poverty, underfunded schools, and the presence of a large, young nonwhite population seems to attract the heavy, discriminating hand of justice. Young people from Oakland are being incarcerated at a disproportionately high rate.

True to form, the county's solution to its juvenile incarceration problem was to build a bigger jail. Only they didn't call it a jail, but a "Juvenile Justice Complex." To replace its 299-bed facility, the county proposed a 540-bed institution, with infrastructure for further expansion. This new complex would be located in the remote eastern edge of the county, far from where the majority of affected families live. Jones spells out the potential consequences:

> The infrastructure and institution of the hall would provide little incentive to reverse the present policy of using detention as a first, not last, resort. Additionally, there would be fewer resources to invest in alternative programs that are more effective in reducing youth crime and recidivism. The relocation of the hall would make it difficult for families and supporters to visit detained children and to appear for court dates and probation meetings where they could advocate for home- or community-based placements. It would also be

more difficult for young people to travel to the new juvenile court, resulting in more "failure to appear" warrants and, ultimately, further increases in detention rates.

To counter this "incarceration agenda," the Ella Baker Center went all out with its Books Not Bars strategy, sponsoring letter-writing campaigns, rallies, meetings with officials, and speaking out at board of supervisors meetings. In partnership with the Youth Force Coalition, it helped organize a concert and educational rally in front of Oakland City Hall, attracting several hundred young people and generating significant media attention.

As the campaign gathered momentum, it began to have an effect. First, in May of 2000, the California Board of Corrections withdrew $2.3 million in preapproved funding from the proposed expansion. Then, in July, the county board of supervisors agreed to reduce the size of the expansion from 540 beds to 360—still a substantial increase over the existing facility.

Meanwhile, EBC sought to enlist every available communications channel to spread the message of the Books Not Bars campaign. To tell the story face to face, it collaborated in producing a youth-oriented education workshop that provided information about the juvenile justice system and encouraged the participants to develop alternatives to incarceration. It set up an Internet listserv and web site; helped produce a twenty-minute video and three public service announcements for cable television; participated in the production of a CD featuring hip-hop entertainers telling the story of the prison/industrial complex in youthful terms, and launched a speaker program for adults aimed at labor, religious, and community organizations.

It worked. Here is how Lenore Anderson describes what she calls "an absolutely fabulous outcome":

> In May of 2003, a member of the county board of supervisors, who had been one of our staunchest opponents, changed his mind. He was now willing to reconsider the issues we had raised and came out publicly to say that he would support a juvenile

hall of only 330 beds and also to keep it in the same town where the current one is located. He then made a motion to that effect and it passed unanimously. So instead of a 540-bed facility all the way out at the eastern edge of the county, the board agreed to build one . . . down the street from the current one.

"It was," she says, "pretty exciting." What she finds even more gratifying are the indications that the turn-around was largely due to EBC's efforts. "When we got involved, the ink was drying on the documents and no member of the board of supervisors showed any interest in even addressing the issues we raised. Only when we generated lots of media coverage and a lot of activism were they forced to pay any attention. We're pretty proud of that," she sums up.

One member of the board of supervisors gives the credit to the active involvement of young people. "I don't think we would be where we are today if it hadn't been for the kids," he says. "They actually worked the system. They were real activists in the democratic process."

Encouraged by this success, the Ella Baker Center is continuing to emphasize the development of "Let's Get Free," a youth-led membership organization. Organizer Nicole Lee succinctly sums up its motivation: "Young people are constantly being criminalized. . . . They're stopped simply because they're young; simply because of the color of their skin; simply because they're poor."

In addition to helping oppose the "super jail," Let's Get Free fought successfully to remove a notorious rogue cop from the streets of North Oakland. Turning their attention to police corruption, they then conducted house visits and street outreach and ran workshops that involved several thousand people. Strategic use of the media—rallies, press conferences, and community forums—triggered enough public scrutiny of police transgressions to force the reopening of several cases in which people had been unjustly arrested. To achieve such successes, the Ella Baker Center trains young people in such skills as writing letters to the editor; being effective media spokespersons; writing press releases, and monitoring issues in the news so they can hold the media accountable for fair reporting.

## A National Solution for a National Problem

Since injustice in the juvenile justice system is obviously not limited to Oakland or even California, EBC is eager to become a resource for interested parties across the country. The Let's Get Free movement, for instance, has spread across the Bay to San Francisco and even to New York City. To support its replication, Ella Baker Center staff has produced a curriculum for the training of youth leaders and set up a student internship program that recruited sixteen high school, college, and law students in 2000.

EBC has also produced a printed report on the Alameda County experience that it has distributed nationwide to media outlets, juvenile justice policy makers, politicians, and some one hundred organizations working on prison issues. Furthermore, it is organizing training sessions for community leaders across the country and distributing a Books Not Bars Action Pack/Organizing Manual.

These national efforts have not, however, distracted EBC from its primary focus on Oakland. Summing up, Van Jones says that the Books Not Bars campaign requires large amounts of research and advocacy, "including many long dry meetings with local officials." While the youth leaders chose the current focus and direction of the campaign, "nevertheless the enthusiasm is not as great as it was during [its] earlier more confrontational or 'active' aspects." Also, since they receive no compensation, volunteers may have to drop out in order to be able to hold a job or take care of family obligations. "We are required to be constantly innovative and creative in our efforts to keep the campaign dynamic and engaging for all the young people involved," Jones adds. "It is a challenging but positive learning experience."

All these efforts have been reinvigorated by the triumphant outcome of the super jail campaign. Lenore Anderson points out that it had a dual significance.

> The campaign stands out not just because of the youth jail issue but also because of criminal justice issues in general. What the campaign did was to demonstrate that it's possible to prevail against the prevalent "you did the crime, you do

the time" attitude. It proved that you can go head-to-head against the "lock-'em-up" sentiment that assumes that the way to keep the community safe is to build bigger jails.

It means that a window has been opened that will enable us to push full force forward and spread the message that what young people really need are "books not bars"; that it's possible to win the hearts of the public with a vision that inspires people, in place of the fear that's been whipped up by the media and conservative policy makers. In Alameda county we shifted the entire public debate in a way that succeeded in changing public policy, and to me that signals that it's possible to effect a climate shift in other places, a shift that is as important as it is exciting.

This is the message, she says, that the Ella Baker Center wants to spread both statewide and nationally:

We want to tell people about the tradeoff between education and incarceration. When you look at other issues—education, workers' rights, health care—you see all kinds of people who are actively organized. But when you look at the incarceration issue, there isn't the same force. That's what we want to generate, setting up campus chapters of Books Not Bars, and helping to create alliances with other groups that want to achieve a shift in budget priorities.

In addition to these efforts to reach a broader base of support, she continues, the center is also attempting to go deeper into the underlying issues:

The way to make progress is to get much more intimately involved in who's getting locked up and why, and then pushing for programs that these youngsters need. You see people getting locked up for school fights instead of getting counseling; getting locked up for being involved with drugs instead of entering a mentoring program. One of the reasons young people get caught up in the justice system is that there is no alternative for them. So we'll not just be saying, "Don't build a bigger juvenile hall"; we will also be saying, "Please build effective drug counseling and mentoring programs. Please start helpful after-school programs." That's what will really make a difference in young people's lives.

Another need is to change public perception. As Vincent Schiraldi, president of the Justice Policy Institute points out, 60 percent of the public thinks that young people account for the majority of violent crimes, when it is actually 15 percent. This misconception may account for much of the willingness of otherwise humane citizens to countenance the mistreatment of teenagers—subjecting them to harassment, arrest, and incarceration that is often marked by humiliation and brutality.

Despite these obstacles, the Ella Baker Center, having tasted victory, persists in its struggles with a sense of optimism. It reflects the spirit of Ella Baker, who said: "Give light and people will find the way." No issue in America today needs that kind of light more than the mistreatment of so many of our younger citizens. EBC's grant from the Veatch Program helps it to lead the way.

# The National Gay and Lesbian Task Force
## Campaigning for Equal Rights

SOFT-SPOKEN, CORDIAL, and informal, David Fleischer does not look like a crusader. In fact, with his gray-tinged beard he might easily be taken for an academic, perhaps a professor of English, an impression reinforced by his articulate manner of speaking and his eloquent writing style. But in fact he is a fighter, and the Goliath this particular David is battling is the powerful and relentless phalanx of those who would deny gay, lesbian, bisexual, and transgender people their basic civil rights. In Oregon there have been thirty-three antigay ballot measures since 1988 and nine in Maine since 1990. In states without ballot referenda, the state legislatures are often just as hostile. In 2004, bills and initiatives opposing same-sex marriage spread like poison mushrooms all over the landscape, and unfortunately many of them passed.

The weapon David Fleischer uses to beat back such attacks is training supporters of the gay, lesbian, bisexual, and transgender (GLBT) community. And in his position as director of organizing and training for the National Gay and Lesbian Task Force (NGLTF), he has trained well over a thousand people in the skills required to succeed. In a bulletin to NGLTF supporters he said: "In tough

237

elections there is no Santa Claus. We have to know who our friends are if we want to win." This strategy often works; most recently, in Miami, where Anita Bryant's 1997 "Save the Children" campaign pioneered antigay ballot initiatives. Fleischer reports on the victory achieved by the SAVE Dade coalition:

> We rewrote a chapter in our movement's history. Together we showed that the majority of voters will vote No to an antigay ballot measure—even though, only a generation ago a vast majority in the same county voted decisively the opposite way. Don't get me wrong. The tactics of fear, dehumanizing, and division still work, and our opposition is masterful at using them. But those tactics no longer prevail when our community runs a strong campaign: 53 percent voted No and 47 percent voted Yes.

First of the four reasons he cites for this success is going door-to-door to identify potential supporters. Here is how he describes one such visit:

> Scene: Me, short, bald, Jewish man at the door, talking to a voter.
>
> "The county Human Rights Ordinance protects all of us from discrimination, whether we're a man or woman, black or white, gay or nongay. Some people want to take the law apart and remove gay people from it. But we think that's wrong— we think everyone should be treated with dignity and respect. What do you think?"
>
> With barely a pause the voter began, "My church said . . ." Oy vay. I figured I knew where we were headed and it wasn't the promised land.
>
> "My church said Jesus loves everybody," she went on. "Discrimination is always wrong."
>
> I went to door number two, said my piece, and the voter immediately began: "My church said," I listened, "homosexuality is a

sin. It's wrong. Read your bible and you'll see the Lord has a plan for a better life for you."

When he stopped talking we paused and looked at each other. Then I said, "Well, I'm gay. I like my life, and if I'm doing a good job at my job, do you think my boss should be able to fire me just because I'm gay?"

The voter was astonished. "Well, of course, no one should fire you for that."

That started a back-and-forth that surprised both of us. We disagreed about why people are gay. But we agreed that discrimination against gays is unacceptable. As he was preparing to read to me from the bible I called a halt, thanked him, and moved to the next door.

Fleischer admits that "there are close-minded homophobes out there," but his door-to-door experience has taught him that there are far fewer than he once thought. And he also stressed that the experience is self-affirming.

Many of us realize early on that we're different, subject to ridicule or hurt. So we crave control as a way to protect ourselves. . . . we build communities and organizations designed to shelter us. But then we miss genuine, reciprocal connection with other people, especially those who aren't just like us. We rarely ask them what they think of us. We assume we know.

We don't ask real questions—like "What do you think?"—we rely on our past experience. . . . We can't forget the feelings we knew when we were young. We can't miss the hostility expressed by right-wing extremists now that we are older. But guess what? Neither has much to do with where most Americans stand today.

In Miami, 88 volunteers from around the country joined the local team in the last two weeks of the campaign. As a result, the SAVE Dade coalition was able to build a list of 74,000 supportive voters, and on election day, a team of seven hundred volunteers staffed the two hundred polling places with the highest turnout, and made 80,000 get-out-the-vote phone calls. They carried the predominantly Anglo precincts by 72 percent to 28 percent, and the black and Caribbean-American precincts by 55 percent to 45 percent. A major contributor to this success was the fact that the leadership team in this ethnically diverse community was roughly 50/50 Hispanic and Anglo, and four out of ten of the NGLTF team members were people of color—an accomplishment, says Fleischer, matched by few bisexual, gay, lesbian, and transgender groups.

The Christian Coalition was one of NGLTF's most emphatic opponents, warning that "homosexualists [sic] want to get orphaned children through adoption…and they're demanding the repeal of all laws that protect children against sexual abuse and exploitation." When the opposing canvassers encountered each other, the "Christians" often took to screaming "God loves you and you're going to hell." It made the campaign, Fleischer says, "exciting, tough—and scary."

## Safeguarding American Values

What made the Miami victory all the sweeter was that it seemed to be part of a watershed development in the battle against antigay initiatives. In 2000, a fairly typical year, the National Gay and Lesbian Task Force lost five such contests and won only one. Then in 2001, for the first time, NGLTF was able to defeat a majority of antigay ballot measures, winning five and losing only two, and in 2002, it won five and lost only one. The reason, a task force analysis concluded, was that by building coalitions with local groups they recruited much larger teams of volunteers, did much more extensive person-to-person campaigning, identified more supportive voters by the thousands, raised tens of thousands more dollars, and turned out many more supporters on election day.

These victories not only boost the morale of the people most directly affected but inspire progressive and marginalized groups of all types that are targets of right wing assault. The task force actually gained enough faith in its organizing skills to help other groups under attack. In the 2003 California plebiscite, for instance, task force staff and volunteers helped to kill Proposition 54, a ballot initiative that would have prevented the state from collecting racial data. The proponents' cynical argument was that gathering such information was racist. In actual fact, state health and education agencies—once deprived of data showing how minority groups were being victimized—would have been unable to implement laws designed to correct such injustices.

Quoting Benjamin Franklin about all hanging together or hanging separately, David Fleischer says,

> All these ballot measures that seek to scapegoat or stigmatize a minority community try to create a political environment that is fundamentally inhospitable to minorities. Some attack immigrants, some attack people of color, some attack gay people—whatever the particular target, these are wedge issues designed to gain or maintain power for the sponsors. It's a good thing that the progressive community has begun to appreciate that we all need to stick up for each other.

NGLTF, therefore, is always looking for allies in its electoral battles, and the issue of fairness is one that knows no political or religious barriers. In both Oregon and Maine, for instance, not only the "usual suspects"—liberal Protestants, Quakers, and Unitarian Universalists—spoke out against antigay ballot measures; so did the local Catholic archbishops.

If they continue to be successful, such alliances may eventually discourage the bigots from using petition initiatives to chip away at the rights of people they don't like. But we're not there yet. As Lorri Jean, then the task force executive director, said in a prescient speech in 2002,

> These fanatics (the right wing) are the people behind the politicians who vocally or quietly oppose our civil rights. These are the people who are promoting anti-GLBT ballot measures all over the country. Once they saw that they were winning with measures to prohibit same-sex marriage, they

decided to cast a wider net. It's not just about same sex marriage any more. Now it's about denying domestic partnership benefits, adoption, foster parenting—it's about the right to be free from discrimination in the workplace, and much more.

If they start losing, the people Jean calls the fanatics may have second thoughts, and our society may some day be cleansed of a particularly vicious and divisive tactic of repression.

## Training Is the Key

The organizing and training department Fleischer heads is the largest NGLTF office, with eight staff members out of a total of thirty. The task force's Veatch application spells out the rationale for this emphasis:

> The fact that the GLBT movement is weak at the grassroots means that politicians—sometimes even our allies—can afford to vote against us, be willing to compromise our rights, or be tepid in their support and not pay a price. . . . That is what the task force is working hard to change with our leadership development, training, and skills building programs, and Policy Institute research and analysis.

Since the task force is not a membership organization, its organizing efforts depend heavily on identifying local groups and individuals who will contribute time and money. It is what Fleischer calls a "talent search." In New Mexico, for instance, he says,

> We probably talked to about 250 people on the phone, telling them about the ballot measure coming up, asking if they were willing to step up to the plate, and asking whether they were interested in training. Then we traveled to New Mexico and, over a period of several weeks, talked in greater depth to everyone who expressed an interest. Then we asked them who else we should be talking to, who has shown some real capability of getting things done.

The thirty-five who agreed to be there then received three-and-a-half days of training on the mechanics of winning an election. While local GLBT groups are the most natural allies for NGLTF, they are not the only ones. In Traverse City, Michigan, for instance, the single most important ally, according to Fleischer, is the local Unitarian Universalist congregation.

Whoever signs up gets training, but Fleischer points out that training is useless if it's never used: "We put so much time and energy into these programs that we need to make sure that the people who come to them are highly likely to put them to use." By following up with participants, NGLTF has established that more than half the people who have taken part in its training programs have subsequently participated in at least one project or election, managed a campaign, or run for office.

## The Broader Implications

The NGLTF is convinced that its electoral successes have implications for all citizens. Because the right wing has spent years building power at the state and local levels, it not only wins ballot initiatives but attracts more and more of its supporters to the polls and thus elects more conservative politicians. This trend, NGLTF points out, affects the broader universe when it comes to causes that progressive, fair-minded people care about. To build countervailing strength, they asked for $75,000 in Veatch funding for the 2003-2004 fiscal year. (They had received $60,000 the year before.)

Fleischer says, "The importance of the Veatch grants is that we've been able to expand the scale on which we do this work, so that now we're able to assist every community that comes under attack, and—most important—we have been able to win the majority of these elections."

Expanding on these comments, Fleischer discusses some of the wider social trends affecting gay, lesbian, bisexual, and transgender people. Regarding the current hot topic of same-sex marriage, for instance, he wonders whether it has helped or hurt the task force's efforts to win community support:

It docs both, really—both helps and hurts. Whatever the issue is, there is always a subtext, and that is whether or not people are willing to treat gay people as human beings. Whether you're talking in the context of marriage, or in the context of nondiscrimination laws, the central difficulty is usually that there is a part of the population who are worried about what they think they know about gay people, and while they may not want to discriminate against them, they're afraid of them. They think that gay people are not like them, that they can't be trusted. A significant part of what we need to do, therefore, is to help people reconsider their stereotypes—the prejudices they grew up with.

This, in addition to soliciting votes, is what makes door-to-door canvassing so important. The moment of truth comes when the canvasser says, "You know, I'm gay," and the householder is suddenly forced to acknowledge that this is a person, not a cartoon figure or a freak. However if the canvasser is straight, it's equally enlightening when he or she says, "You know, I'm not gay, but I have a lot of gay friends and I think they deserve the same rights as you or me."

"When there's somebody on their doorstep," Fleischer explains,

There is a reality of someone not so different from them and it doesn't jibe with the image in the back of their heads, which is not a very flattering picture. In our society, it's not often that somebody comes up to you and expresses sympathy for gay people or even uses the word "gay." It's not what most people experience. It means that the rights of gays is not a big issue in most people's lives. They're much more concerned with whether the car is going to start tomorrow. But once they think about it, when they consider that there are human consequences to their voting decision, then they begin to see the issue through a different lens. Obviously, not everyone then agrees with us, but increasingly they do.

It's possible, he believes, that the recent trend of portraying gay people on hit television shows is contributing to this shifting of stereotypes.

> Even though the characters on *Will and Grace* or even *Queer Eye for the Straight Guy* are also stereotypes, at least they show images that are significantly kinder than many people's worst fears. Those fears are based on the assumption that gay people are really not in any way like them. Then they watch somebody on TV and they realize, well, you know, there's not really this total disconnect between them and the people I care about.

There may be a parallel, Fleischer thinks, between these shows and what *The Cosby Show* did for the image of blacks or, before that, the Goldberg programs for the public perception of Jews.

> Almost every minority community in America has been marginalized, and while these shows certainly didn't put an end to bias, they at least were part of the process of people being accepted as people, leading the same kind of lives as everybody else. Probably they made it easier for the majority to start thinking of Jews and African Americans as not so different from themselves, instead of fitting some stereotype they grew up with. Neither is *Will and Grace* going to solve the problem. There's a huge amount of work we still have to do. But does it make it easier or harder? I think it probably makes it easier.

Another issue that concerns Fleischer is that gay and lesbian activism remains predominantly a "white" phenomenon.

> There are very few places around the country where the gay, lesbian, bisexual, and transgender community has built deep and broad cross-racial relationships. Of course that's a reflection of the larger culture, but it seems that the gay community is not any more evolved on matters of race. The truth is that there are not enough data for us to know, but it's

my impression that in most communities there are networks
of black and Latino and Asian as well as white gay people,
but that these networks are separate from each other. A substantial part of what we want to accomplish, therefore, is to
help leaders in these various communities forge relationships across racial lines and build multiracial teams. It's very
damaging for our community that these relationships don't
usually exist, just as it is damaging for American society at
large that people of different races spend so little time
together and know so little about each other.

Speaking of the lack of data, he adds that there are not even
reliable data on how many GLBT people there are in the United
States today:

It all depends on how you count. Is your definition of a gay
person someone who is self-identified as gay? Someone who
regularly has sex with people of the same sex? Or who has ever
had sex with someone of the same sex? It's quite possible that
the vast majority of people of any race who have sex regularly
with people of the same sex don't identify themselves as gay
and don't participates in gay communities or institutions.

The only way that's going to change is if the stigma attached to
being gay is reduced. Only then will people feel free to honestly
indicate not only to others but to themselves that they are gay,
and there will no longer be this disconnect between how people wish to be identified and how they in fact lead their lives.

When that happens, perhaps there will also no longer be
media coverage that ridicules gay people and portrays them as
freaks. Fortunately, most media coverage these days is about
the election activities we carry on, and the more we do a really
good job, the more likely are we to attract fair press coverage.

Like all marginalized and disadvantaged groups in this country, the GLBT community cannot succeed in its battles for fair
treatment without the help of allies who are motivated by a sense
of justice and a passion to turn the best of America's vision into

day-to-day reality. Among such allies, David Fleischer says he sees the Veatch Program as an outstanding example.

Veatch and the Unitarian Universalist Congregation at Shelter Rock have made some very unusual and admirable choices. It strikes me that the animating philosophy of Veatch and the congregation has been to think seriously about how to reduce and, if possible, eliminate the divisions in our society that polarize us and keep us from understanding each other in our common humanity. That is not a common approach. It certainly is not a popular approach because it has required Veatch to embrace communities that are not popular. Its willingness to do that is ultimately going to mean that people will look back on what it has accomplished and applaud it not just for being important and wise, but courageous.

At Passover, friends and I use a Haggadah that is called *Neged Hazarem*. It's named after a newspaper published in the Warsaw ghetto. It means "against the current." It is very difficult to stand against the current, especially in these retrograde political times. What a strange thing that we live in a time when reflection on our shared humanity requires standing against the current. But Veatch has been willing to stand for these values, and I think there will be a time in the future when the values for which Veach has taken its stand will be broadly shared.

# Jubilee USA
## *Wiping Out Odious Debt and HIV/AIDS*

IF ANTIGAY PREJUDICE is toxic in America, it has proved deadly in Africa. While by no means all of the AIDS/HIV epidemic is due to same-sex transmissions, that perception in sub-Saharan countries is so widespread and the taboo about homosexuality so strong that people would rather risk death than come out to be tested and treated. Compounding the problem is the burden of debt that keeps many countries from funding adequate public health programs.

Since the Veatch Program does not fund overseas organizations, none of its grants go to Africa, but it does support Jubilee USA, which, in turn, is part of an international network that is trying to get rich nations to cancel ruinous, third world debt. Jubilee USA members include churches and other religious communities, labor unions, AIDS activists, trade campaigners, and environmental groups, plus more than 8,000 individuals. By giving to Jubilee USA, Veatch supports the effort to correct a basic economic problem that contributes heavily to African poverty, the "odious debt" that cripples many African countries.

The classic pattern is as follows. A dictator of a poor country borrows money far in excess of what the local economy can afford, using the money to build himself palaces, stuff Swiss bank accounts, and buy armaments for purposes of repression or aggression. The lenders, eager for profits, choose to ignore the borrower's unpalatable reputation and poor credit rating.

If the dictator is eventually overthrown, the country is stuck with these noxious loans; then on the edge of default, it applies for relief to one of the two primary international lending institutions—the World Bank and the International Monetary Fund (IMF). The bailout takes place, but frequently lenders require the debtor nation to accept conditions that force it to cut public expenditures, thereby crippling its health care and education systems.

Its mission, says Jubilee USA, is to put an end to this devastating cycle. As its funding proposal to the Veatch Program explains,

> Today international debt has become a new form of slavery. Debt slavery means impoverished people and nations are denied their sovereign right to determine their economic future and to have access to basic human services. Through harmful conditions wealthy nations have used debt as an instrument. . . . forcing [countries] to adopt policies that directly benefit creditor nations at the expense of human development.

The proposal goes on to cite specific examples of how public debt hurts ordinary people:

- Nicaragua was forced to cut education spending by two-thirds. In Tipitapa, to cite one community, where there were eighty-four free public schools ten years ago, there is only one today. Even so, the IMF has suspended further debt relief for Nicaragua for not having cut public spending even further.

- In Malawi, one child in four does not live to see his or her fifth birthday. But Malawi is denied debt relief because IMF and the World Bank blame the government for not making deeper cuts in social services.

- Zambia has been spending $150 million a year in debt service, and by 2004 payments were scheduled to climb to more than $200 million. To meet these payments Zambia has to borrow even more, leaving next to nothing to fight the AIDS pandemic which has cut life expectancy to thirty-eight years.

As the Zambian example illustrates, there is a direct connection between the debt burden and the AIDS epidemic. Jubilee USA national coordinator, Marie Clarke, comments,

> Debt is the lens through which we come to our work, although for the last couple of years we have increasingly been working on the connections between debt and health issues, especially the AIDS epidemic. . . . The way debt impacts health is the pivotal issue, because debt impacts access to treatment, access to medication, and the health services in impoverished countries. Then the economic consequences of the health crisis further exacerbate the debt burden.

Clarke became active in the movement first as a volunteer and then as a member of the board of directors. In 2001 she started as one of two full-time staff members. They have their work cut out for them. *The Guardian* of London, cites a report by the World Development Movement about Senegal:

> It tells a depressingly familiar tale of a debt-stricken country in West Africa forced to adopt the full range of stabilization measures prescribed by the IMF and World Bank: cuts in public spending, tight monetary and fiscal policies, exported growth, trade and investment liberalization, deregulation of internal prices, dismantling of the public sector, privatization of state-owned enterprises, the rolling back of the state and the abrogation of the right to control its own economic destiny. [These policies have] deprived peasants of their livelihood, [raised] the percentage of the population that is

malnourished . . . and [left] 80 percent of people living on less than $2 a day.

Responding to this worldwide crisis, the U.S. Congress voted in May 2003 to double the amount of debt relief previously awarded, specifying that it would be free from IMF austerity measures. Unfortunately, six months later the Treasury Department, in what would appear to be a clear violation of the will of Congress, was still resisting implementation of the legislation.

Would debt relief ease the burden of HIV infection? Bill Ferguson of Jubilee USA answers that question in an op-ed article in the San Jose *Mercury News*:

Africa last year [2002] alone spent $14 billion in debt service, while millions died of AIDS. The UN estimates that $10 billion yearly is needed to fight AIDS in Africa. If a moratorium on debt repayments were implemented by the world's most powerful nations, Africa's own resources could then be freed up to fight the devastating plague.

Instead, as Muthoni Wanyeki of the African Women's Development and Communications Network points out, "Africa has paid our debts three times over in the last ten years alone. Today we are three times as indebted as we were ten years ago." This in a continent that is "ground zero" of the global HIV/AIDS crisis, with an estimated 75 percent of the sub-Saharan population infected and mostly left untreated, at least in part due to lack of funds.

The World Trade Organization (WTO) compounds the debt burden on impoverished nations by insisting that they lower their trade barriers, remove subsidies, and privatize public services as a condition of joining. Often these so-called structural adjustment programs leave poor nations unable to negotiate reciprocal relief by their trading partners. A frequently cited example of this one-sided situation is the way the United States subsidizes its cotton farmers to the extent that peasant growers in Africa, unable to compete, are driven into bankruptcy. European sugar subsidies have a comparable effect.

## Working Together

Founded in 1997, the Jubilee USA network has some seventy member organizations. Among the most active participants are the Evangelical Lutheran Church of America; the Presbyterian Church USA; the Episcopal and Methodist churches; Oxfam USA; the AFL-CIO; and many community-based groups and local congregations. Member organizations are expected to make a financial contribution and to attend the biannual meeting of the Network Council, which in turn elects the fifteen-member Coordinating Committee—in effect, its board of directors. Veatch also supports the Fifty Years Is Enough Network, an allied organization that is not faith-based; both are based in Washington, D.C.

Jubilee USA derives its name and inspiration from a biblical passage that describes a jubilee when those enslaved because of debt were freed and land lost due to debt was returned. In contemporary terms, according to the network's mission statement, it is an alliance that is

> Building a grassroots movement to achieve the complete cancellation of debts owed by impoverished nations, and an end to unjust economic policies imposed on those nations. Working in solidarity with partners around the world, Jubilee USA promotes its mission through public education, grassroots organizing, media outreach, policy analysis, and advocacy.

Jubilee USA draws heavily on the expertise and resources of its member organizations, especially in the preparation of its educational materials. For the most part, this presents no problems because all the members share the basic commitment that the debt burden needs to be lifted, and the Network Council is thus able to arrive at consensus positions fairly easily. On only a few issues is there a difference of opinion, most notably regarding trade. "We've got some very challenging disputes going on as to the most appropriate way to address trade issues," Clarke concedes. On one side are those who believe that all trade barriers and subsidies should be lifted;

on the other those who are convinced that some international markets need continued protection. Until such differences are resolved, the network is unable take an official position. What it can and does do, Clarke says, is to focus on educating people about the connections between trade and debt—a proposition all members accept.

Empowered by this consensus, Jubilee USA has scored some encouraging successes. For instance, regarding the problems created by the IMF and World Bank structural adjustment programs, the network has been able to put so much pressure on these institutions, as well as on the WTO, that, according to Clarke "they have been shamed into seeing the need to revise some of their policies."

## An International Effort

Since the IMF, World Bank, and WTO are all international organizations, they are susceptible to pressure from Jubilee chapters around the world. There are active groups in the United Kingdom, Germany, and Norway, as well as in Asia, Africa, and Latin America. The British group nowadays concentrates on research and data collection, a resource widely used in other countries. And while each of the individual Jubilee campaigns acts pretty much on its own initiative, they do discuss common goals and strategies. In October 2003, Jubilee leaders from the northern hemisphere met with those from the south in Argentina, and the southern group has elected an international Coordinating Committee.

In the United States, the current emphasis is on grassroots activism. Clarke gives an example:

> When we're trying to influence Congressional action, instead of focusing our energies on Washington, we try to involve our supporters all over the country to take a stand in favor of or against certain policies. There are times when we still interact directly with members of Congress, as we did with the debt relief bill this May [of 2003] to double the amount of debt relief, but we really prefer to influence them by building a broader movement that changes public opinion.

In line with that tactic, Jubilee USA has decided not to spend as much time cultivating national newspapers such as the *Washington Post* or the *New York Times*, and instead to encourage its local supporters to engage with their hometown media, offering them media training as well as policy statements, suggested op-ed articles, and editorials they can adapt.

There is also a new program called "Jubilee Congregations," designed to get not just national denominations, but their local constituents to become active, with the national office providing speakers for adult education and social justice events. Grassroots activism also produced the "snowing of Snow"—John Snow, the secretary of the treasury was inundated with eleven thousand postcards asking him to follow through with the legislative mandate to reduce the debt burden. In response, the Treasury Department felt compelled to raise the issue with the IMF and the World Bank, but it may take some time to find out how they will respond. "These institutions are not very transparent," Clarke points out, "and we will depend on leaked documents to know whether or not the Treasury Department actually did what they were instructed to do."

Jubilee also hopes that the members of Congress who got the bill passed will hold hearings at which Snow will be challenged as to whether or not he obeyed the law. The hope is that once the legislation is implemented, the burden of debt service will be cut from $2 billion a year to $1 billion. However, the best available estimate of the resources actually flowing out of impoverished countries—a figure far beyond just debt service—is $3 billion.

One sign that the pernicious effect of odious debt is becoming more widely understood is the outcome of the Senate vote on the Bush Administration's proposed $20.3 billion reconstruction allocation for Iraq. Many opponents of the war, as well as senators concerned about the ballooning national debt, wanted to make part of the aid package a loan. Despite the political appeal of this proposal, it was beaten back by senators who realized that it might well destabilize whatever democratic government eventually emerges.

Jubilee USA, which considered the loan provision "a disaster of an idea" supports the cancellation of Iraq's debt. In addition to helping the new Iraqi government, Jubilee says,

> This cancellation would for the first time define in U.S. law the concept of odious debt, establishing a strong precedent in our own legal system. It would also enhance the efforts of our partners around the globe to establish the precedent more firmly in international law. Perhaps that would discourage future lenders from propping up dictators and tyrants who use the money to exploit their own people.

Two historical precedents suggest that the battle for debt forgiveness may have implications beyond the obvious humanitarian aspects. After World War I, the Allies exacted heavy financial penalties on Germany, a policy that undermined the new Republic and quite likely helped bring the Nazis to power. After World War II, on the other hand, the victors helped with the reconstruction of their defeated enemies, and both Germany and Japan have enjoyed mostly stable and peaceful governments ever since.

Perhaps some day we can say the same about Iraq and admire how African governments, able to spend their resources on the health and welfare of their people, are coping with the AIDS epidemic. If so, the Jubilee movement will deserve a fair measure of the credit and supporters of the Veatch Program will know that they did their share.

# The Long Island
# Unitarian Universalist Fund
## *A Denominational Commitment*

THE GRANTS DESCRIBED so far go to organizations in just about every corner of the country. Cynics might say that's typical of liberals: They are all for social reform on Indian reservations or in some inner city, while they themselves live in segregated or even gated communities. The Congregation at Shelter Rock and its Veatch Program not only defy this stereotype; they have gone out of their way to initiate social justice programs close to home by launching and supporting the Long Island Unitarian Universalist (LIUU) Fund. Started in 1993, the fund received $340,000 in 2002.

Not that that was the first time Veatch had committed itself to promoting justice in its own backyard, but while previous support from Veatch and the Shelter Rock congregation had gone directly to grassroots and social service organizations, now funding decisions are made by the Long Island UU Fund, which embraces other Nassau and Suffolk County UU congregations. When the fund receives a grant proposal that requires further study, it enlists its UU advisory committee in a site visit. The seven-member committee is made up of representatives from seven Unitarian Universalist congregations on Long Island, exclusive of Shelter Rock. The link with

Shelter Rock is made personal once a year, however, when the fund presents a Sunday service at the congregation, entitled "UU Principles in Action: Promoting Social Change on Long Island."

Among its major accomplishments in 2002, the LIUU Fund lists these as primary:

- Creating an islandwide movement to support the development of affordable housing.

- Supporting a grassroots movement, in cooperation with the Nature Conservancy, to protect the water resources of Long Island's South Fork.

- Helping immigrants, single parents, farm workers, and the victims of medical malpractice.

- Developing role models for youth and providing them with training as organizers and activists.

These highlights hardly encompass all of the fund's activities. When the community of Farmingville was torn apart by hate groups campaigning against immigrant laborers, Darren Sandow, the fund's program officer, organized a coalition to address the crisis. This project developed into a full-blown community organizing effort that successfully drafted and passed a county bill to protect day laborers, which regrettably was vetoed by the then Suffolk County executive. Finally, after two Mexican immigrants were nearly beaten to death, Sandow raised the money to form and support the Long Island Immigrant Alliance, made up of some twenty community, religious, labor, and immigrant organizations.

In Sandow's words, "Strategic grant making involves supporting social change projects that address the true needs of a community, that have the backing and involvement of a solid constituency, and that take into account other similar efforts across Long Island or across the nation." To find out where its support can do the most good, he spends much of his time visiting community leaders and attending local civic and issue-oriented group meetings. In the town of Riverhead, for instance, such contacts led to the creation of a community group that seeks to revitalize its downtown and to implement smart growth strategies. In another instance, he cofounded a coalition of more than fifty childcare providers and supporters who are working to improve the quality of early childcare islandwide.

When Paul Glatzer of the UU Fellowship at Stony Brook finished his three-year term on the advisory committee, he wrote, "For me, this has been a most rewarding experience, to be able to see firsthand how grants to local grassroots organizations can be such effective catalysts for change—for positive change—here on Long Island. . . . The LIUU Fund is clearly a successful example of [our] being able to put faith into action."

Action, in contrast to the common "not in my backyard" reaction, specifically focused on Shelter Rock's backyard.

The initiative for involving neighboring Unitarian Universalist congregations was strongly supported by executive director Marjorie Fine. While not herself a Unitarian Universalist, Fine is very intentional in making Veatch grants reflect the denomination's traditions and ideals. She introduced the policy that each time a program officer recommends approval of a grant, he or she is asked to specify which of the principles of the Unitarian Universalist Association the grant is intended to implement.

Fine traces her commitment to liberal religious principles to her own background. "I was the product of very liberal Jewish parents," she explains, "and we thought that the system could be fixed and that it was the responsibility of all of us to make that happen. It came across in our Jewish values and also in our belief in democratic principles. As my father used to say, 'You can't be an armchair activist.'"

After getting a degree in social work, with a focus on community organizing, she worked on behalf of reproductive rights, went on to teach fundraising to chapters of the National Council for Jewish Women, and became a development director and later executive director for a New York City public charity. This experience led to a board seat of a foundation that "was teaching people who had inherited wealth, and who at first wanted to reject this 'dirty money,' to hold on to it and do good things with it for social justice."

She started to work for Veatch in 1993.

"I knew that Veatch had a great reputation for doing social justice work and for being very smart. I also knew that getting a Veatch grant is like getting a *Good Housekeeping* seal of approval, serving as a good sign for other funders as well."

In addition to serving as the primary liaison between the staff and the Veatch board of governors, Fine supervises the program officers and support staff, and takes direct responsibility not only for denominational grants but also for the area of progressive philanthropy, where—as described in the chapter "Helping the Helpers"—she is an active participant and leader.

That completes the story of how Caroline Veatch's initially modest bequest has transformed a congregation and a denomination, and has become a critically important counterforce in a nation that is in danger of betraying its basic principles of democracy and justice. All that is left is to add a few words about the personal impact of piecing the story together.

# Whose America Is It?

ADMIRATION. ANGER. Determination. Pride. And hope.

These were the emotions triggered by working on this book.

Admiration for what one Unitarian Universalist congregation has achieved in translating its commitment to our denomination's principles into effective action.

Anger at hearing firsthand the stories of injustice and unfairness inflicted on the poor and powerless in our society.

Determination to tell their stories as accurately as possible so that others will join in the effort to right these wrongs.

Pride in being part of a religious family whose ideals have inspired the long record of generosity of the Unitarian Universalist Congregation at Shelter Rock.

And, finally, the hope that others may be encouraged to follow their example, for on this hope hinges nothing less than the future of our country.

That is because the enterprise of which Veatch is a small but important part is nothing less than the struggle to determine whether or not we as Americans will continue to live up to our nation's founding ideals. You might well call this the true patriotism.

As of the end of 2004, the outcome of that struggle is very much in doubt. As William Sinkford, UUA's president, has said: "There is a war being fought for the soul of America. . . . It is being fought on Capitol Hill and in state legislatures, in school boards and in zoning hearings. It is a war whose outcome will answer the question: *Whose America Is It?*"

The Veatch Program is in the forefront of that struggle. Its commitment is well summed up in its 2002 annual report:

> Much is wrong in the world as we find it in the beginning of the twenty-first century. Tremendous wealth and greed exist alongside unbearable poverty; we find little compassion and almost no greatness among our national leaders. We believe that fundamental changes are needed—changes in values, in priorities, in analysis, and in governance.
>
> We also believe that these changes will occur only if the people of this country themselves provide the leadership that is so sorely lacking. The Veatch Program funds organizations of people, not of "experts," because we believe that it is only by rebuilding democracy in this country from the bottom up that new policies will be envisioned, demanded, and implemented. . . .
>
> As an essential part of rebuilding our democracy, the Veatch Program supports organizations that teach people the skills that have been lost as they have been systematically excluded from the political process: public speaking, conducting meetings, raising money, challenging bureaucrats, and holding political representatives accountable.
>
> [In line with] the principles of Unitarian Universalism, we strive through our grantmaking to encourage "a free and responsible search for truth and meaning; justice, equity, and compassion in human relations; and the use of the democratic process."

Unfortunately, there are also powerful forces arrayed against these principles, and too many well-intentioned Americans are indifferent to or unmindful of what is at stake. That is why it is so encouraging and so important that the Veatch Program and all who have made it possible have chosen to use the legacy of Caroline Veatch to join the battle on the right and—let us hope—the winning side.

# Veatch Program
# Funding Guidelines


THE UNITARIAN UNIVERSALIST Veatch Program at Shelter Rock supports programs that foster the growth and development of the denomination and that increase the involvement of Unitarian Universalists in social action.

It also supports nondenominational organizations whose goals reflect the principles of Unitarian Universalism. The Veatch Program's nondenominational grantmaking is limited to U.S.-based organizations with a locus of activity in the United States.

Support is generally provided only to nonprofit, tax-exempt organizations as defined under section 501(c)(3) of the United States Internal Revenue Code. The Program does not make grants to individuals or government institutions, nor is funding provided to nondenominational organizations for capital projects, endowments, annual contribution drives, historic preservation, direct services, scientific or academic research, film or video production, publications, or cultural activities.

Veatch operates its grantmaking program with seven staff people supporting the work of an all-volunteer board. Of the more than 850 proposals it receives each year, more than 200 receive funding and many of these are renewals.

The majority of Veatch grants are made for a period of one year. Grant requests are not considered from organizations with a current

Veatch grant or from organizations that have failed to comply with reporting requirements or other conditions of a previous Veatch grant. Organizations with a current grant from the Unitarian Universalist Funding Program or a current grant from the Long Island Unitarian Universalist Fund are also not eligible.

In its annual report, the Veatch Program lists its grants under the following categories: Unitarian Universalism; Civil and Constitutional Rights; Environmental Justice; Capacity Building for Social Justice, including infrastructure, media and communications, and progressive philanthropy; Economic Equity and Democracy; Poverty, Jobs, and Welfare Reform; Workplace Organizing; Making Democracy Work, including community organizing and democratic participation; and finally a group of grants in the New York Metropolitan Region.

For application procedures, please visit the UU Veatch Program Web site at *www.uucsr.org/veatch/funding_guidelines.htm.*

# Acknowledgments

I WOULD LIKE to express my thanks and appreciation to everyone quoted or cited in this book. Their generosity in sharing their time and insights during the interviews on which this work is based are what made it possible. In addition, many of them provided me with reports, copies of their grant applications to the Veatch Program, and other documents that were of essential help. Thanks, too, to Bob Sunley, chair of the Shelter Rock congregation's archives and history committee whose suggestion initiated this project. Others whose backup and encouragement I greatly appreciate include Mary Benard, my ever-helpful editor, and her support staff at Dartmouth Publishing, including Lydia Horton and Elizabeth Hopwood. Finally, though first in my sense of gratitude, I am indebted to Marjorie Fine and her staff at the Veatch Program for their patience in responding to my repeated requests for information and source material. They not only made the preparation of the manuscript possible, they made it a pleasure. This book was funded, in part, by the Fund for Unitarian Universalism.

In addition I made use of various printed sources. Two can be obtained from bookstores by those who would like to do further reading: *Fast Food Nation* by Eric Schlosser, and *South Bronx Rising* by Jill Jonnes.

Others that are not so easily available are reports and self-published volumes, and I am grateful to all who made them available. While not a complete list, they include: *Faith-Based Community Organizing*, published by Interfaith Funders; *Exemplary Grantmaking* and *Payout for Change*, by J. Gillenkirk, published by the National Network of Grantmakers; two Beacon Press publications— *Going Public*, by Michael Gecan, and *Beacon 150: A Brief History of the Beacon Press*, by Susan Wilson; Interfaith Funders' Annual Reports; *Privatization & Contracting Out*, edited by Jack Metzgar and published by the Midwest Center for Labor Research; *Changing the Political Culture of the Texas Border*, by George Rips, published by the Texas Center for Policy Studies; an article by William G. Sinkford in *UU World* titled "Our Calling"; *25 Years of Organizing*, edited by Alicia Hernández and published by the Southwest IAF Network; and *Sacred Waters/El Agua es de Todos*, published by the Southwest Network for Environmental & Economic Justice.

W. R.

# Index

501s, 23

ACORN. *See* Association of
　Community Organizations for
　Reform Now
Acree, Robin, 73, 75
Adelaide (Australia), 33–34
Adelman, Robert, 4, 5, 28
AFL-CIO, 205, 253
Africa, 43, 154, 249, 251, 252, 254
African Women's Development and
　Communications Network,
　252
Agriculture, Department of, 79, 84
AIDS, 23, 249, 251, 252, 256
Al Inshirah Islamic Center, 68, 69
Alabama Arise
　fighting predatory lending, 126–127
　focus on legislature, 122–126
　overview, 121–122
Alaska, 39, 152
Alaskan Communities Against
　Persistent Organic Pollutants
　(POPS), 152

Albuquerque, 142–146
Alinsky , Saul, 50, 51, 173, 186
All Souls Church, 36, 67, 68, 69, 70, 71
Allende, Dana Jordan, 122, 123
Alliance for Justice (AFJ), 11, 21–25
Alliance School Initiative, 191
Allison, Roger, 77, 78, 82
Allstrom, Louise, 34, 35
Allstrom, Mark, 33, 34
Almanza, Susana, 130, 131, 133, 135,
　136, 138
American Federation of
　Government Employees, 91
American Friends Service
　Committee, 90
American Nazi Party, 77
American Postal Workers, 90
American Unitarian Association
　(AUA), 2, 5, 32, 38
Ameriquest Mortgage, 63
Amkar, Mohammed, 35
Anaya, Carmen, 187, 196
Anaya, Eddie, 188
Anderson, Lenore, 229, 231, 233